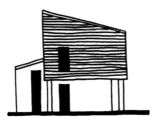

THE HOME BOOK

KÖNEMANN

is an imprint of
Frechmann Kolón GmbH
www.frechmann.com

© 2014 for this edition: Frechmann Kolón GmbH

Editorial project: LOFT Publications
Barcelona, Spain
Tel.: +34 932 688 088
Fax: +34 932 687 073
loft@loftpublications.com
www.loftpublications.com

Editorial coordination:
Simone K. Schleifer

Assistant editorial coordination:
Aitana Lleonart

Editor and Texts:
Mariana R. Eguaras Etchetto

Art director:
Mireia Casanovas Soley

Design and layout coordination:
Claudia Martínez Alonso

DTP Designer:
Ignasi Gracia Blanco

Translations:
Equipo de Edición, Barcelona
Rachel Sarah Burden (English),
Katrin Kügler (German),
Elke Doeiman (Dutch),
Sophie Lechauguette (French)

Published in the United States in 2014 by:

Skyhorse Publishing
307 West 36th Street, 11th Floor
New York, NY 10018, USA
T: +1 212 643 6816
info@skyhorsepublishing.com
www.skyhorsepublishing.com

Published in Asia in 2014 by:

PAGE ONE

Page One Publishing Pte Ltd
20 Kaki Bukit View
Kaki Bukit Techpark II
Singapore 415956
T: +65 6742 2088
F: +65 6744 2088
enquiries@pageonegroup.com
www.pageonegroup.com

ISBN 978-3-86407-209-3
ISBN 978-981-4523-10-3 (Page One Publishing)
ISBN 978-1-63220-593-3 (Skyhorse, USA)

Printed in Spain

Building a house is a decision which is complicated by a multitude of factors, and governed by the budget available to carry out the project. The same applies when considering renovating a home, whether because the family is growing or simply to change one's environment. Even during periods of economic instability, refurbishing a house can be cathartic, as it is not always necessary to spend large sums of money to create new, more comfortable and pleasing surroundings.

As Albert Einstein said, "from crisis is born invention, discovery and great strategies: creativity is born". Why not make the most of a time of change to renovate one's home and, by association, oneself?

The first things to be taken into account when building or remodeling a house is the space: the number of square meters in each area, how rooms are to be used and the relationship between them. The function of each room is important when selecting materials which will be suitable and attractive. It is also important to choose the style of decoration according to the possibilities offered by the spaces.

Several of these decisions can be resolved by choosing a particular material for the flooring or the wall coverings in the chromatic tone wanted for the room, or by the use of specific lighting to create the desired effect.

Selecting lighting, colors, materials, furnishings and accessories according to one's needs and personality will turn a house into a home – a space created by the residents as an oasis to enjoy.

Prendre la décision de construire une maison serait simple si de multiples facteurs ne venaient compliquer les choses, à commencer par le budget disponible pour mener le projet à bien. C'est exactement pareil quand on envisage de rénover ou transformer un logement existant parce que la famille s'agrandit ou pour changer d'environnement. Même en période d'incertitudes économiques, refaire la décoration peut être une occupation salutaire. Il n'est pas toujours nécessaire d'engloutir des sommes énormes pour créer un intérieur à la fois au goût du jour et plus agréable à vivre.

Comme le disait Albert Einstein, «l'inventivité, les découvertes et les grandes stratégies naissent de la crise, c'est ainsi qu'apparaît la créativité». Alors pourquoi ne pas profiter d'une période de mutation pour renouveler son chez-soi, et se réinventer par la même occasion ?

Avant d'entreprendre de construire ou de modifier, il faut commencer par prendre la mesure de l'espace disponible. Quelle est la surface des pièces ? Quelle sera leur destination et comment y vivrez-vous ? La fonction de chaque pièce conditionne en partie les matériaux, qui seront choisis pour être plaisants et pratiques. Les volumes disponibles vont eux aussi influer sur le style de la décoration pour créer une harmonie.

Le choix des revêtements de sol et des murs, puis celui de la gamme chromatique, sont les premières décisions à prendre – avant d'envisager les éclairages qui feront ressortir les nuances choisies pour obtenir l'effet recherché.

Lumière, couleurs, matériaux, mobilier et accessoires, soigneusement sélectionnés selon vos désirs et votre personnalité, transformeront n'importe quel lieu en un petit paradis, créé à l'image de ses habitants pour leur plus grand bonheur.

Der Bau eines Heims ist mit komplexen Entscheidungen verbunden, die von vielfältigen Faktoren sowie den für den Erbau des Hauses veranschlagten Geldmitteln abhängig sind. Dies trifft auch zu, wenn wir einen Umbau ins Auge fassen, sei es aufgrund einer Familienerweiterung oder aus dem Wunsch nach einer Veränderung. Sogar in wirtschaftlich instabilen Zeiten kann die Erneuerung unseres Zuhauses einen erfrischenden Neuanfang darstellen, denn die Schaffung einer neuen Umgebung, die uns größere Bequemlichkeit bietet und uns mit Freude erfüllt, ist auch ohne große Geldinvestition möglich.

Wie schon Albert Einstein meinte, «ist die Krise die Geburtsstunde des Erfindungsgeistes, der Entdeckung, und der großen Strategien, jene der Kreativität». Warum also sollten wir die Gelegenheit zur Veränderung unseres Heims nicht nutzen, und uns gleichzeitig auf den neuesten Stand bringen?

Der erste Schritt bei der Errichtung oder des Umbaus unseres Zuhauses besteht in der Überlegung, welcher Raum uns zur Verfügung steht: die Quadratmeterzahl der einzelnen Räume, wofür wir sie nutzen und wie wir sie miteinander in Verbindung setzen wollen, sind ausschlaggebend. Der Verwendungszweck eines jeden Raumes ist entscheidend für die Wahl der Materialien, die für ihn am besten geeignet sind und daher in ihm am besten zur Geltung kommen. Auch den Dekorationsstil, der von den Möglichkeiten abhängig ist, die uns die verschiedenen Räume bieten, müssen wir von Anfang an in Betracht ziehen.

Viele dieser Fragen können durch die Wahl eines bestimmten Materials für den Boden und die Wandverkleidung gelöst werden, sowie durch die Entscheidung für eine bestimmte farbliche Tonalität, die wir einem Raum verleihen wollen oder aber auch für eine bestimmte Beleuchtung, um einen gewünschten Effekt zu erzielen.

Die Wahl der Beleuchtung, der Materialien, der Möblierung und der Accessoires für unseren Wohnraum sind von unseren Bedürfnissen und unserer Persönlichkeit abhängig und machen aus diesem Wohnraum unser Zuhause, einen Raum, den wir geschaffen haben und in dem wir uns wohlfühlen, unsere persönliche Oase.

Bij het besluit over te gaan tot het bouwen van een huis spelen talloze factoren een rol, maar worden de meeste keuzes bepaald door het beschikbare budget. Datzelfde geldt wanneer u overweegt een huis te verbouwen vanwege gezinsuitbreiding of gewoon om van 'omgeving' te veranderen. Zelfs in periodes van economische onzekerheid kan het opknappen van een woning de moeite waard zijn, want het is niet altijd nodig grote sommen geld uit te geven om een nieuwe en aangenamere leefomgeving te creëren.

Zoals Albert Einstein ooit zei: "Uit een crisis ontstaan uitvinding, ontdekking en grootse strategieën: er ontstaat creativiteit." Waarom zou u niet het beste maken van een tijd van verandering om uw huis en daarmee uzelf te vernieuwen?

De eerste dingen waarmee u rekening moet houden bij het bouwen of verbouwen van een huis is de beschikbare ruimte: het aantal vierkante meters in elke ruimte, de functie van de vertrekken en hun onderlinge relatie. De functie van elk vertrek is van belang bij het kiezen van materialen die geschikt en mooi zijn. Het is ook belangrijk dat u de stijl van de inrichting afstemt op de mogelijkheden die de ruimte biedt. Verschillende van deze beslissingen kunnen worden opgelost door een bepaald materiaal te kiezen voor de vloer- of wandbekleding, in de gewenste kleur voor het vertrek, of door het gebruik van specifieke verlichting om het beoogde effect te bereiken.

Door zelf de verlichting, kleuren, materialen, meubels en accessoires te kiezen naar uw eigen behoeften en persoonlijkheid maakt u van een huis een thuis - een ruimte die door uzelf is gecreëerd als een oase om van te genieten.

Construir una vivienda es una decisión compleja de abordar por la multitud de factores que se deben tener en cuenta, además del presupuesto con el que contamos para llevar a cabo la edificación de una casa. Lo mismo sucede cuando consideramos necesaria una reforma, sea porque la familia se amplía o porque deseamos darle un nuevo aire al hogar. Incluso en épocas de inestabilidad económica, remodelar nuestra casa puede resultarnos catártico, ya que no son necesarias grandes inversiones de dinero para generar un nuevo entorno que nos proporcione mayor comodidad y placer.

Como dijo Albert Einstein, «en la crisis nace la inventiva, el descubrimiento y las grandes estrategias; nace la creatividad». ¿Por qué desaprovechar un momento de cambio para renovar nuestro hogar y, por extensión, actualizarnos?

Los primeros factores que debemos considerar a la hora de construir o remodelar nuestra casa es el espacio de la vivienda: la cantidad de metros cuadrados que tienen cada uno de los ambientes, qué uso le daremos a estas habitaciones y cómo deseamos relacionar los espacios entre sí. Tendremos en cuenta la funcionalidad de cada estancia para seleccionar los materiales que mejor se adapten y que más destaquen. Asimismo, también deberemos elegir de antemano el estilo de decoración, según las posibilidades que nos ofrezcan estos espacios.

Varias de las respuestas a estos interrogantes se pueden resolver con la elección de un determinado material para el pavimento y el revestimiento de las paredes, a través de la tonalidad cromática que queramos imprimir en un ambiente o con la aplicación de una iluminación específica para lograr un efecto deseado.

Elegir la luz, los colores, los materiales, el mobiliario y los complementos para la casa en función de nuestras necesidades y la personalidad hará que se convierta en un hogar, en un espacio de y para nosotros, en un oasis para disfrutar.

L'edificazione di una casa è una decisione alquanto complessa da prendere a causa della gran quantità di elementi di cui si deve tener conto, oltre al budget di cui si dispone per realizzarla. La stessa cosa accade quando riteniamo necessario effettuare una modifica, una ristrutturazione, per il fatto che la famiglia s'ingrandisce o perché desideriamo dare un nuovo aspetto al nostro rifugio. Incluso in epoche di instabilità economica, restaurare la propria casa può risultare un fatto catartico, giacché non è necessario investire grosse somme di denaro per creare un nuovo ambiente più comodo e gradevole.

Come ha detto Albert Einstein, «dalla crisi nascono l'inventiva, le scoperte e le grandi strategie; nasce la creatività». Per quale ragione dunque dovremmo sprecare un momento di cambiamento per rinnovare la nostra casa e, per estensione, aggiornare noi stessi?

Il primo elemento che dobbiamo considerare per costruire o restaurare la nostra casa è lo spazio: la quantità di metri quadrati occupata da ogni ambiente, quale uso daremo alle stanze e come vogliamo mettere in relazione gli spazi tra loro. Terremo conto della funzionalità di ogni stanza per scegliere i materiali più adatti e più belli esteticamente. Inoltre, dovremo scegliere a priori lo stile dell'arredamento, in base alle possibilità che ci offrono questi spazi.

Diverse soluzioni a tali questioni si possono raggiungere tramite la scelta di un determinato materiale per il pavimento e per il rivestimento delle pareti, attraverso la tonalità cromatica che desideriamo dare a un ambiente o con l'applicazione di una particolare illuminazione per ottenere un effetto voluto.

Scegliere la luce, i colori, i materiali, l'arredamento e gli accessori per la casa in base ai nostri bisogni e alla nostra personalità farà sì che la nostra casa diventi una dimora accogliente, uno spazio personale fatto per noi, un'oasi in cui passare magnifici momenti.

Além da questão do orçamento com que contamos para levar a cabo a edificação de uma casa, construir uma vivenda é uma decisão de abordagem complexa, devido aos incontáveis factores a ter em consideração. O mesmo sucede quando sentimos a necessidade de uma mudança de edifício, tanto porque a família aumenta como porque queremos ter um lar com outro ar. Em períodos de instabilidade económica, pode ser catártico remodelarmos a nossa casa, uma vez que criar ambientes novos que nos proporcionem mais comodidade e prazer não exige necessariamente grande investimento em dinheiro. Tal como disse Albert Einstein, «é na crise que nascem as invenções, os descobrimentos e as grandes estratégias; nasce a criatividade». Que razão pode haver para não aproveitarmos uma época de mudança para renovarmos o nosso lar e, por extensão, nos actualizarmos?

O primeiro factor que devemos considerar no momento de construir ou remodelar a nossa casa é o espaço habitável: a quantidade de metros quadrados de cada um dos ambientes, a utilização a que se destina cada divisão e como pretendemos articular os vários espaços entre si. Teremos em conta a funcionalidade de cada aposento para seleccionarmos os materiais que melhor se adaptem e que mais se destaquem. Por outro lado, também devemos escolher de antemão o estilo da decoração, de acordo com as possibilidades que cada espaço nos proporcione.

Algumas destas questões podem ser resolvidas escolhendo um determinado material para o pavimento ou para o revestimento das paredes, uma tonalidade cromática para criarmos um determinado ambiente ou usando uma iluminação específica para conseguir o efeito desejado.

A escolha da luz, das cores, dos materiais, do mobiliário e dos complementos para a casa em função das nossas necessidades e personalidade fará com que esta se transforme num lar, num espaço de e para nós próprios, num oásis de prazer.

Att bygga hus är ett beslut som kompliceras av en mängd faktorer och som styrs av den budget som är tillgänglig för att genomföra projektet. Detsamma gäller för att renovera ett hem, oavsett om det är därför att familjen växer eller enbart för att förändra sin omgivning. Även under perioder av ekonomisk instabilitet kan det vara renande att renovera ett hus eftersom det inte alltid är nödvändigt att spendera stora summor pengar för att skapa nya, bekvämare och tilltalande omgivningar.

Som Albert Einstein sa: "ur kris föds uppfinning, upptäckt och bra strategier, kreativiteten är född".

Varför inte göra det mesta av förändringens tid att renovera sitt hem och sig själv i samband med det?

De första sakerna att ta med i beräkningen när man bygger eller omskapar ett hus är utrymmet: antalet kvadratmeter i varje utrymme, hur rummen ska användas och förhållandet mellan dem. Varje rums funktion är viktig när man väljer material som kommer att vara lämpliga och tilltalande. Det är också viktigt med inredningsstil i enhet med möjligheterna som utrymmet erbjuder.

Många av dessa beslut kan lösas genom att välja ett visst material till golvläggning eller väggbeklädnad i den färgnyans som önskas till rummet, eller genom att använda specifik belysning för att skapa önskad effekt.

Genom att välja ljussättning, färger, material, möbler och accessoarer enligt sina behov och sin personlighet förvandlas ett hus till ett hem – ett utrymme skapat av de boende som en oas att njuta av.

FAMILIARLOFT

GIOVANNI GUIOTTO/INDESIGN ARCHITETTURA E DISEGNO INDUSTRIALE
© Matteo Piazza

Through the careful distribution of space, within the ambiguity characteristic in a loft, this property combines the privacy and flexibility necessary for a family of five. The spaces are large, with a five meter high ceiling and a predominance of white.

Grâce à une distribution de l'espace particulièrement soignée, avec l'ambiguïté caractéristique d'un loft, cette demeure dose savamment besoins d'intimité et de convivialité nécessaires au bien-être d'une famille de cinq personnes. Les volumes sont vastes, le plafond est à cinq mètres de hauteur et le blanc est dominant.

Dem typisch undefinierten Charakter eines Lofts wurde die klare Einteilung des Raums entgegengesetzt, wodurch die für eine fünfköpfige Familie nötigen Privatbereiche sowie Flexibilität geschaffen wurden. Der gesamte, großzügig angelegte Raum wird von einem fünf Meter hohen Dach bedeckt, an dem die weiße Farbe hervorsticht.

Door de zorgvuldige verdeling van de ruimte, met de voor een loft kenmerkende ambiguïteit, combineert deze woning de privacy en flexibiliteit die nodig zijn voor een gezin van vijf. De ruimtes zijn groot, met een 5 meter hoog plafond en veel wit.

A través de una precisa distribución del espacio, dentro de la ambigüedad típica de un loft, se combinaron la privacidad y la flexibilidad necesarias para una familia de cinco miembros. Todo el espacio goza de un generoso volumen con un techo de cinco metros en el que predomina el color blanco.

Attraverso una precisa distribuzione dello spazio, pur mantenendosi nella tipica ambiguità che caratterizza i loft, si è riusciti a unire la privacy e la flessibilità necessarie per una famiglia di cinque persone. Tutto lo spazio presenta un abbondante volume con un soffitto di cinque metri in cui predomina il colore bianco.

Através de uma distribuição precisa do espaço na ambiguidade típica de um loft, combinou-se a privacidade e a flexibilidade necessárias para uma família de cinco membros. O espaço goza de um volume generoso, sobretudo graças a um pé direito de cinco metros de altura, em que predomina o branco.

Genom noggrann fördelning av utrymmet, inom den ambiguösa karaktären för ett loft, kombinerar denna fastighet avskildheten och flexibiliteten som är nödvändig för en familj på fem. Utrymmena är stora, med ett fem meter högt innertak och dominans av vitt.

DURAN LOFT

JAIME GAZTEL
© Antonio Corcuer

This collection of double-storey lofts has an eye-catching façade which contrasts with the simple bricks that cover the rest of the exterior. Although the uneven street means that each of the blocks can easily be differentiated, the distinction has been emphasized by the chromatic pattern.

Cet ensemble de lofts en duplex se caractérise par une façade qui attire tous les regards tandis que les autres murs extérieurs sont faits de simples briques. Du fait de la pente de la rue, il est facile de distinguer les différents bâtiments, mais l'emploi de la couleur souligne l'individualité de chaque immeuble.

Diese doppelhohen *Lofts* stechen durch ihre originelle Fassade hervor, die sich von der umliegenden, mit einfachen Ziegelsteinen realisierten Außenfassade, abhebt. Obwohl das Gefälle der Straße die optische Unterscheidung der einzelnen Blöcke leicht macht, wollte man diese noch zusätzlich durch ein Farbenspiel betonen.

Deze reeks tweelaags lofts heeft een oogstrelende voorgevel die contrasteert met de eenvoudige stenen die de rest van de buitenmuren vormen. Hoewel de blokken makkelijk van elkaar te onderscheiden zijn door de aflopende straat, wordt de scheiding benadrukt door het kleurenpatroon.

Este conjunto de *lofts* de doble altura llama la atención por su original fachada, que contrasta con los sencillos ladrillos que cubren el resto del exterior. A pesar de que el desnivel de la calle permite diferenciar visualmente cada uno de los bloques, se ha querido enfatizar esta distinción con el juego cromático.

Questo insieme *loft* a doppia altezza attrae l'attenzione per la sua facciata originale, la quale crea un netto contrasto con i semplici mattoni che ricoprono il resto degli esterni. Nonostante il fatto che il dislivello della via permetta di distinguere visivamente ogni blocco, si è voluto dare enfasi questa differenza mediante il gioco cromatico.

Este conjunto de *loft* com dois níveis chama a atenção pela originalidade da fachada, que contrasta com os tijolos simples que cobrem as restantes paredes exteriores. Apesar de o desnível da rua permitir distinguir perfeitamente cada um dos blocos, pretendeu-se destacar es diferença com o jogo cromático.

Denna samling av tvåvåningsloft har en iögonenfallande fasad som kontrasterar mot de enkla tegelstenar som täcker resten av exteriören. Även om den ojämna gatan innebär att vart och ch av kvarteren lätt kan urskiljas har distinktionen framhävts av det kromatiska mönstret.

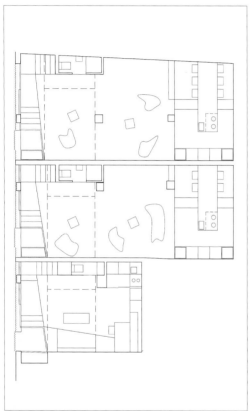

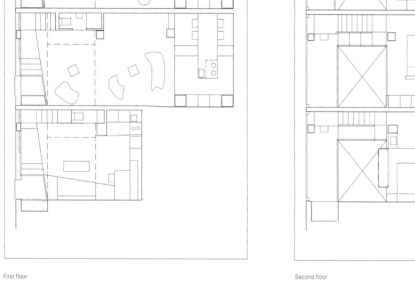

First floor

Second floor

CANAPOST HOUSE

LIZARRITURRY TUNEU ARQUITECTURA
© José Luis Hausmann

Built on a lot close to the historic center of a small village in Empordà, Spain, this project was developed around a large property built from recovered old brick. The ceilings are made with large rafters in whitened French oak, in the same way as old hangers.

Bâti dans une propriété proche du centre historique du petit village d'Empordà, en Espagne, ce projet consistait à imaginer une vaste demeure construite en vieilles briques. Les plafonds sont agrémentés de grands chevrons de chêne blanchi.

Das auf einem in der Nähe des historischen Kerns eines kleinen Dorfes im Empordà errichtete Projekt wurde um eine große, aus wieder verwerteten Altziegeln gefertigte Halle herumgebaut. Die Decke wird von Balken aus gebleichtem französischen geblichenen Ahorn getragen.

Dit pand staat op een kavel dicht bij het historische centrum van een klein dorpje in Empordà in Spanje en is gebouwd rond een groot gebouw van oude bakstenen. De plafonds zijn gemaakt van grote daksparren van gewit Frans eikenhout.

Construida en un terreno próximo al centro histórico de un pequeño pueblo del Empordà, el proyecto se ha desarrollado alrededor de una gran nave realizada con ladrillo antiguo de recuperación. Los techos se han construido con grandes cerchas o encaballadas de madera de roble francés blanqueado, a la manera de los antiguos hangares.

Costruita su un terreno nei pressi del centro storico di un paesino della regione dell'Empordà, questa casa è stata sviluppata intorno a un grande capannone realizzato con mattoni antichi recuperati. I tetti sono stati costruiti con grandi centine o giunzioni di legno di rovere francese sbiancato, come si usava una volta per gli hangar.

Construída num terreno próximo do centro histórico de uma aldeia do Empordà, na Catalunha, o projecto desenvolveu-se em redor de uma grande construção com tijolo antigo recuperado. Os tectos foram construídos com grandes asnas ou encaballadas de madeira de carvalho francês branqueado, à maneira dos antigos hangares.

Detta projekt, byggt på en jordlott nära det historiska centrat i en liten by i Empordà i Spanien, utvecklades kring en stor egendom byggd av återvunnet gammalt tegel. Innertaken är gjorda med stora taksparrar i vitnad fransk ek, på samma sätt som gamla hängare.

CABRILS-LOMBAO HOUSE

EMMA HAUSMANN (stylist)
© José Luis Hausmann

This newly built house in a residential area of Barcelona is distributed over two and a half storeys in order to continue the uneven effect of the surroundings. The light colored marble tiles in the living room and the dark marble tiles in the dining room create a perfect combination with the decoration.

Cette maison récente construite dans une zone résidentielle de Barcelone comporte un étage et demi pour respecter l'esprit de cet environnement fort irrégulier. Contrastant avec le sol sombre de la salle à manger, les dalles en marbre clair du salon s'accordent parfaitement à la décoration.

Es handelt sich um ein neu erbautes Einfamilienhaus, das sich in einem Wohnviertel in Barcelona befindet, seine Räumlichkeiten verteilen sich über zweieinhalb Etagen, die das der Umgebung eigene Gefälle weiterführen. Die hellen Marmorfliesen im Wohnzimmer und die dunklen im Esszimmer ergeben zusammen mit der Dekoration ein perfektes Bild.

Dit pas gebouwde huis in een woonwijk in Barcelona is verdeeld over tweeënhalve verdieping om het ongelijkmatige effect van de omgeving voort te zetten. De lichte marmeren tegels in de woonkamer en de donkere marmeren tegels in de eetkamer combineren perfecte met de inrichting.

La casa es una torre unifamiliar, de nueva construcción, edificada en una zona residencial de Barcelona, y está distribuida en dos plantas y media para continuar con la sensación de desnivel propio del entorno. Las baldosas de mármol claro en el salón y las de mármol oscuro para el comedor crean una combinación perfecta con la decoración.

La casa è una villa unifamiliare, di recente costruzione, edificata in una zona residenziale di Barcellona, ed è distribuita su due piani e mezzo per non interrompere la sensazione di dislivello tipica della zona. Le piastrelle di marmo chiaro nella sala e quelle di marmo scuro per la sala da pranzo danno luogo a una perfetta combinazione con l'arredamento.

Esta casa unifamiliar de construção nova foi edificada numa zona residencial de Barcelona e está distribuída por dois andares e meio para dar continuidade à sensação de desnível do meio que a envolve. O pavimento de mármore claro na sala de estar e de mármore escuro na sala de jantar combinam perfeitamente com a decoração.

Detta nyligen byggda hus i ett villaområde i Barcelona är fördelat på två och ett halvt plan för att fortsätta med omgivningarnas ojämna verkan. De ljusa marmorplattorna i vardagsrummet och de mörka marmorplattorna i matrummet skapar en perfekt kombination med inredningen.

HILL SIDE RESIDENCE

HAYBALL LEONARD STENT, SUE CARR
© Shania Shegedyn

This family home in a suburb of Melbourne affords a magnificent view of the Yarra River. The building was constructed in the old garden of the neighboring property, which provided the architects with a double challenge: to create a design which was suitable for the steep slope and to integrate the new property with the surrounding buildings.

Cette maison familiale située dans une banlieue de Melbourne a une superbe vue sur le fleuve Yarra. Elle a été construite sur une partie de l'ancien jardin de la propriété voisine, ce qui présentait une double difficulté pour les architectes. Ils durent imaginer un plan qui convienne à la forte pente tout en permettant à la nouvelle construction de s'intégrer aux bâtiments l'entourant.

Dieses in einem Vorstadtviertel von Melbourne angesiedelte Einfamilienhaus bietet eine wundervolle Aussicht auf den Yarra Fluss. Das Gebäude wurde im ehemaligen Nachbarsgarten erbaut, wobei die Architekten eine doppelte Hürde zu meistern hatten. Der Entwurf musste an das steile Gefälle angepasst werden und das Projekt sollte harmonisch in die bereits bebaute Umgebung eingebunden werden.

Deze gezinswoning in een buitenwijk van Melbourne kijkt uit op de rivier de Yarra. Het huis is gebouwd in de voormalige tuin van het pand ernaast, wat de architecten een dubbele uitdaging opleverde: een ontwerp te maken dat geschikt was voor de steile helling en aansloot bij de omringende gebouwen.

Esta vivienda unifamiliar, en un suburbio de Melbourne, ofrece una magnífica vista del río Yarra. L estructura se levantó en el antiguo jardín de la propiedad vecina y el desafío de los arquitectos fu doble: sortear con el diseño la empinada cuesta e integrar este edificio en el entorno ya construido

Quest'abitazione unifamiliare, in un suburbio di Melbourne, offre una magnifica vista del fiume Yarr La struttura è stata edificata nell'antico giardino della vicina proprietà e la sfida che hanno dovut accettare gli architetti è stata doppia: da un lato la necessità di evitare, mediante il progetto, il ripid pendio e, dall'altro, quella di inserire armoniosamente questo edificio nell'ambiente circostante.

Esta casa unifamiliar de um subúrbio de Melbourne oferece uma vista magnífica sobre o rio Yarr A estrutura foi erigida no antigo jardim da propriedade vizinha e o desafio dos arquitectos foi dupl compensar a vertente íngreme e integrar a construção no entorno já edificado.

Detta familjehus i en förort till Melbourne skänker en storslagen utsikt över Yarra-floden. Byggnade konstruerades i den intilliggande egendomens gamla trädgård, vilket försåg arkitekterna med e dubbel utmaning: att skapa en design som var lämplig för den branta sluttningen och att integrer den nya egendomen med de omkringliggande byggnaderna.

Ground floor

First floor

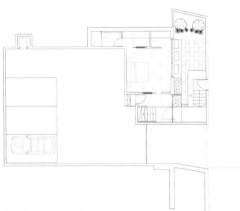

Basement

THE BOW QUARTERS

YANIK ALLARD ARCHITECTURE & DESIGN
© Carlos Domínguez

This apartment is located on the second storey of an old match factory, built at the end of the 19th century, in London. The renovation aimed to create a large, open space, and so the bedroom was placed on a 'floating' upper level. The dark parquet gives the space depth and sophistication.

Cet appartement londonien est au deuxième étage d'une ancienne manufacture d'allumettes du XIXe siècle. La rénovation visait à créer un vaste espace ouvert, aussi les chambres ont-elles été placées en mezzanine sur un niveau supérieur. La coloration sombre du parquet fait ressortir la profondeur sophistiquée de l'espace.

Das Gebäude befindet sich im zweiten Stock eines Londoner Gebäudes, über einer ehemaligen Streichholzfabrik, die Ende des 19. Jahrhunderts erbaut wurde. Mit dem Umbau sollte ein großer, offener Raum entstehen, daher wurde das Schlafzimmer auf einer schwebenden höheren Ebene situiert. Der dunkle Parkettboden verleiht den Räumen Tiefe und Erlesenheit.

Dit appartement bevindt zich op de tweede verdieping van een oude, eind 19e eeuw gebouwde luciferfabriek in Londen. Bij de verbouwing is getracht één grote, open ruimte te creëren en daarom kwam de slaapkamer op een 'zwevende' verdieping. Het donkere parket geeft de ruimte diepte en raffinement.

Situado en la segunda planta de un edificio londinense, el apartamento se encuentra en una antigua fábrica de fósforo construida a finales del siglo XIX. Con la remodelación se quiso lograr un gran espacio abierto y por eso se situó el dormitorio en un nivel superior flotante. El parqué oscuro da profundidad y sofisticación a los ambientes.

Questo appartamento si trova al secondo piano di un edificio londinese, un'ex fabbrica di fosforo costruita alla fine del XIX secolo. Con la ristrutturazione si è voluto ottenere un grande spazio aperto e per questa ragione è stata posta la camera da letto a un livello superiore. Il parquet oscuro conferisce profondità e uno stile sofisticato agli ambienti.

Situado no segundo andar de um edifício londrino, o apartamento encontra-se numa antiga fábrica de fósforos construída em finais do século XIX. Com a remodelação, pretendeu-se criar um espaço aberto grande, pelo que se deslocou o quarto de dormir para um nível superior flutuante. O soalho escuro confere profundidade e sofisticação aos ambientes.

Denna våning ligger på andra våningen i en gammal tändsticksfabrik, byggd i slutet av 1800-talet, i London. Renoveringen syftade till att skapa ett stort, öppet utrymme, därför placerades sovrummet på ett "flytande" övre plan. Den mörka parketten ger utrymmet djup och raffinemang.

Fourth floor

Mezzanine

BEGUR

ANTONI MASÓ/MANUFACTURING ARCHITECTURE SERVICES ORGANIZATION; SILVIA RADEMAKERS (stylist)
© José Luis Hausmann

The project aimed to make the most of the property's location on a cliff on the Spanish Costa Brava, close to Begur. It was designed so that all the rooms, including the private areas, had views of the sea, and ensured the arrangement of the space on the single storey was practical, simple and logical.

Ce projet visait à tirer le meilleur parti de la situation de cette propriété au sommet d'une falaise sur la Costa Brava, près de Begur. La maison a été conçue de sorte que toutes les pièces sans exception aient vue sur la mer, et que l'organisation de l'espace sur un étage soit pratique, simple et logique

Bei diesem Projekt hat man versucht, seinen Standort – es befindet sich auf einer Klippe an der spanischen Costa Brava in der Nähe von Begur – maximal zu nutzen. Es wurde so geplant, dass alle seine Räume (Privaträume inklusive) Ausblick aufs Meer gewähren, außerdem ist deren Anordnung äußerst praktisch und einfach gestaltet und folgt der natürlichen Reihenfolge, in der sie normalerweise auch begangen werden.

Dit project beoogde de locatie van het pand op een klif aan de Spaanse Costa Brava, in de buurt van Begur, optimaal te benutten. Het is zo ontworpen dat alle ruimtes, ook de privévertrekken, uitkijken op de zee en dat de indeling van de ruimte op de enkele verdieping praktisch, eenvoudig en logisch is.

El proyecto buscaba aprovechar el emplazamiento de la vivienda, ubicada sobre un acantilado en la Costa Brava española, cerca del cabo Begur. Se diseñó de tal forma que todas las dependencias tuvieran vistas al mar –incluso las áreas privadas– y una distribución práctica, sencilla y de circulación coherente en una única planta.

Il progetto ha voluto sfruttare la posizione della casa, che sorge su una scogliera della Costa Brava spagnola, nei pressi di capo Begur. A tale scopo, tutte le sue parti sono state pensate in modo tale da avere la vista sul mare -perfino le zone private- nonché una distribuzione pratica, semplice e con una circolazione coerente in un solo piano.

O projecto pretendia aproveitar a localização da vivenda, situada sobre uma falésia na Costa Brava espanhola, perto do cabo Begur. Foi desenhada de forma a conseguir que todas as divisões tivessem vista para o mar — incluindo as áreas privadas — e uma distribuição prática, simples e de circulação coerente num único piso.

Projektet siktade på att få ut det mesta av egendomens placering på en klippa på spanska Costa Brava, nära Begur. Det designades så att alla rum, inklusive de privata delarna, hade havsutsikt och såg till att dispositionen av utrymmet på det enda planet var praktisk, enkel och logisk.

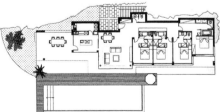

Plan

CHET BAKERSTRAAT

HOFMAN DUJARDIN ARCHITECTEN
© Matthijs van Roon

This apartment was completely renovated with a new distribution of the space and an innovative design which also includes the furnishings and lighting system. The flooring is resin and tiles, with rugs of different colors and textures completing the decoration.

Cet appartement a été entièrement rénové. L'espace a été redistribué selon un design novateur qui englobe le mobilier et l'éclairage. Les sols en résine et carrelage sont ponctués de tapis de couleurs et textures différentes qui complètent le décor.

Dieses Appartement wurde von Grund auf renoviert und der zur Verfügung stehenden Raum völlig neu geplant und gestaltet, auch die Einrichtung und Beleuchtung wurden miteinbezogen. Am Boden sind das Harz und die azulejos (farbigen Fliesen) bemerkenswert; die mehrfarbigen, verschiedenartig gewobenen Teppiche vervollständigen die Dekoration.

Dit appartement is volledig gerenoveerd, met een nieuwe ruimte-indeling en een innovatief ontwerp dat ook het meubilair en de verlichting omvat. De vloeren zijn afgewerkt met kunsthars en tegels; vloerkleden in verschillende kleuren en texturen maken de inrichting af.

Este apartamento fue totalmente renovado con una nueva planificación del espacio y un innovador diseño que también alcanzó al mobiliario y al sistema de iluminación. En el pavimento destaca la resina y los azulejos; las alfombras de diferentes colores y texturas completan la decoración.

Questo appartamento è stato completamente rinnovato mediante una nuova pianificazione dello spazio e un design innovativo che ha interessato anche l'arredamento e il sistema d'illuminazione. Sul pavimento spiccano la resina e le piastrelle e, in ultimo, sono stati posti tappeti di vari colori.

Este apartamento foi totalmente renovado com uma nova planificação do espaço e um design inovador que também abarcou o mobiliário e o sistema de iluminação. No pavimento, destaca-se a resina e os azulejos; tapetes de várias cores e texturas completam a decoração.

Denna våning var helt renoverad med ny planlösning och en innovativ design som också inkluderar möbleringen och ljussättningssystemet. Golvet är laminat och plattor, med mattor i olika färger och kvaliteter som kompletterar inredningen.

1. Entry
2. Kitchen
3. Dining room
4. Living room
5. Terrace
6. Bedroom
7. Bathroom
8. Toilet

Plan

CUPITOL HOUSE

EDUARDO A. RIBEIRO, MANUEL R. ANTUNES
© Pedro D'Orey

The very uneven ground where this house is located determined the design of the property on two levels, to adapt to the configuration of the terrain. The idea was to create the simplest shape possible, with clearly defined lines and spaces which harmonize with the surrounding countryside.

La forte déclivité du terrain sur lequel cette maison a été construite a déterminé son plan sur deux étages, conçu pour suivre la configuration du site. L'idée était de créer la forme la plus simple possible, avec des lignes clairement définies et des espaces en harmonie avec le paysage environnant.

Die Unebenmäßigkeit des Grundstücks, auf dem dieses Gebäude errichtet wurde, führte zu einem zweistöckigem Entwurf, der sich an die Beschaffenheit des Bodens anpasst. Es sollte eine möglichst einfache Form entstehen, ihre Linien sollten klar definiert sein und mit der landschaftlichen Umgebung harmonisieren.

De zeer ongelijkmatige ondergrond waarop dit huis is gebouwd, was bepalend voor het ontwerp van het pand op twee niveaus, aangepast aan het terrein. Het idee was om een zo eenvoudig mogelijke vorm te creëren, met uitgesproken lijnen en ruimtes die harmoniëren met het omringende landschap.

El terreno muy irregular donde está emplazada esta vivienda determinó el diseño de un volumen en dos niveles para adaptarse a la configuración del suelo. La idea fue crear una forma lo más simple posible, con líneas claramente definidas y espacios que armonizasen con el paisaje circundante.

Il terreno molto irregolare su cui è stata edificata questa casa ha obbligato a progettare un volume disposto su due livelli in modo da adattarsi alla configurazione del suolo. L'idea è stata quella di creare la forma più semplice possibile, con linee chiaramente definite e spazi in armonia con il paesaggio circostante.

A irregularidade do terreno em que esta vivenda se encontra determinou o desenho de um volume em dois níveis para se adaptar à configuração do solo. A ideia foi criar uma forma o mais simples possível, com linhas claramente definidas e espaços que estivessem em harmonia com a paisagem envolvente.

Den mycket ojämna marken där detta hus är beläget bestämde designen på huset på två plan för att anpassa det till terrängens form. Tanken var att skapa enklast möjliga form med klart definierade linjer och utrymmen som harmonierar med den omgivande landsbygden.

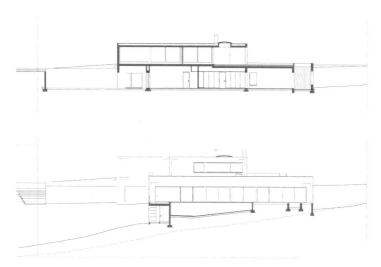

Elevations

Ground floor

PARK WEST APARTMENT

BONETTI/KOZERSI STUDIO
© Matteo Piazza

Imposing spaces dominate this house, putting more emphasis on horizontal than vertical lines. The furnishings, and the few decorative elements with their Asian inspiration, come together with the light colors throughout the interior - on ceilings, walls and floors - to create a feeling of calm and freedom.

Les espaces imposants qui dominent dans cette demeure font davantage ressortir l'impact des lignes verticales que celui des horizontales. Les meubles et les quelques éléments décoratifs d'inspiration asiatique forment un bel ensemble qui se détache sur le fond de couleurs claires retenu pour les plafonds, les murs et les sols. Il s'en dégage une atmosphère de liberté apaisante.

Beeindruckende Räumlichkeiten charakterisieren diese Wohnung, die Betonung liegt auf eher auf den horizontalen als den vertikalen Linien. Das Mobiliar und die wenigen, asiatisch anmutenden dekorativen Elemente vermitteln zusammen mit den hellen Farben des gesamten Innenraums -Decken, Wände und Böden - ein Gefühl der Freiheit und Gelassenheit.

Imposante ruimtes bepalen de sfeer in dit huis en leggen meer nadruk op horizontale dan op verticale lijnen. Het meubilair en de paar decoratieve, oosters aandoende elementen scheppen in combinatie met de lichte kleuren een gevoel van rust in het hele interieur - op plafonds, wanden en vloeren.

Imponentes espacios predominan en esta vivienda y ponen más énfasis en la horizontalidad que en las líneas verticales. El mobiliario y los pocos elementos decorativos y de inspiración asiática, sumados a los colores claros de toda la estructura interior -techos, paredes y suelos-, brindan una sensación de calma y libertad.

Quest'abitazione è dominata da imponenti spazi che danno una maggiore enfasi all'orizzontalità piuttosto che alle linee verticali. L'arredamento e i pochi elementi decorativi d'ispirazione asiatica, sommati ai colori chiari di tutta la struttura interna -soffitti, pareti e pavimenti-, offrono una sensazione di calma e libertà.

Neste apartamento, predominam os espaços imponentes que dão mais protagonismo à horizontalidade do que às linhas verticais. O mobiliário e os poucos elementos decorativos e de inspiração asiática, em harmonia com as cores claras da totalidade da estrutura interior - tectos, paredes e pavimentos -, proporcionam uma sensação de calma e de liberdade.

Imponerande utrymmen dominerar detta hus där de horisontella linjerna framhävs mer än de vertikala. Möblerna och de få dekorativa elementen med sin asiatiska inspiration förs samman med de ljusa färgerna som är genomgående i inredningen - på tak, väggar och golv - för att skapa en känsla av lugn och frihet.

Plan

REINA VICTORIA APARTMENT

INÉS RODRÍGUEZ / AIR PROJECTS
© Jordi Miralles

The entrance and staircase were the central architectural elements on which the renovation of this house was based. The white walls create unity and continuation between the two levels. The flooring was treated in order to maintain the original wood, and some areas are defined using rugs.

L'entrée et l'escalier sont les éléments architecturaux centraux autour desquels a été conçue la rénovation de cet intérieur. Les murs blancs assurent l'unité et la continuité entre les niveaux. Les parquets ont été traités de façon à préserver les bois d'origine, certains espaces étant définis au moyen de tapis.

Die Renovierung des Wohnraums setzte am Vorraum und den Stiegen an. Die weißen Wände lassen die beiden Stockwerke ineinander übergehen und einheitlich erscheinen. Die Böden wurden behandelt, um ihr Originalholz zu erhalten, einige Bereiche wurden durch die Anbringung von Teppichen begrenzt.

De entree en de trap waren de centrale bouwkundige elementen waarop de verbouwing van dit huis is gebaseerd. De witte wanden scheppen eenheid en continuïteit tussen de twee niveaus. De originele vloer is gerestaureerd en sommige plekken zijn geaccentueerd door middel van vloerkleden.

El vestíbulo y la escalera fueron los elementos arquitectónicos centrales sobre los que se basó la renovación de la vivienda. Las paredes blancas proveen unidad y continuidad a ambas plantas. Se trataron los pavimentos para mantener la madera original y se delimitaron algunos ambientes por medio de alfombras.

Il vestibolo e la scala sono stati gli elementi architettonici centrali intorno ai quali si è proceduto a realizzare la ristrutturazione dell'abitazione. Le pareti bianche danno unità e continuità a entrambi piani. I pavimenti sono stati trattati in modo da conservare il legno originale e alcuni ambienti sono stati delimitati mediante l'uso di tappeti.

O vestíbulo e a escada foram os elementos arquitectónicos centrais que geriram a renovação do apartamento. As paredes brancas conferem unidade e continuidade a ambos os pisos. Os pavimentos foram tratados para manter a madeira original e alguns ambientes foram delimitados através de tapetes.

Entrén och trappan var de centrala arkitektoniska element på vilka renoveringen av detta hus baserades. De vita väggarna skapar enhet och kontinuitet mellan de två planen. Golvet behandlades för att underhålla originalträet och några områden definieras av mattor.

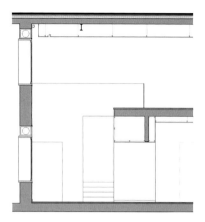

Entrance

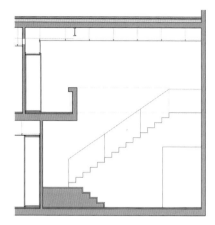

Stairs elevation

Lower level

Upper level

HOUSE IN **TELLURIDE**

JOHN PAWSON
© Undine Pröhl

Telluride is an old village which became a mining community. Today it is a National Historic District and a cultural point of interest also popular with tourists. Given its historical character, urban development laws are in place to conserve the existing countryside, so it was decided to build a simplified version of the traditional two-storey house with a garage at one end.

Telluride est un vieux village qui est devenu le centre d'une communauté minière. Il fait aujourd'hui partie d'une zone historique classée, un lieu de mémoire en même temps qu'un site touristique. Compte tenu de son caractère historique, la réglementation locale en matière de construction est très restrictive afin de préserver le caractère du paysage. Il a donc été décidé de construire une interprétation simplifiée de la maison traditionnelle à un étage avec un garage d'un côté.

Telluride, ein einstmaliges Indianerdorf und späteres Bergbaugebiet, steht heutzutage unter Denkmalschutz, es zieht zahlreiche Besucher an und steht im Mittelpunkt kulturellen Interesses. Aufgrund seines historischen Charakters ist die Erhaltung seiner Landschaft bauschriftlich festgelegt. Hier entschied man sich für eine vereinfachte Version des klassischen zweistöckigen Hauses mit einer angebauten Garage.

Tellirude is een oud dorpje dat een mijnwerkersgemeenschap is geworden. Nu is het een culturele trekpleister die ook populair is onder toeristen. Gezien het historische karakter van het dorp is er sprake van een beschermd dorpsgezicht; daarom is besloten een eenvoudige versie van het traditionele tweelaagse woonhuis met een garage opzij te bouwen.

Telluride es un antiguo pueblo indígena y posterior campamento minero, que hoy en día es Distrito Histórico Nacional y foco de interés turístico y cultural. Debido a su carácter histórico, la conservación de los paisajes existentes es una norma urbanística. Aquí se optó por una versión simplificada de la casa tradicional de dos pisos con un garaje en un extremo.

Telluride era un antico villaggio indigeno, divenuto in seguito campo di minatori, e oggi è un Distretto Storico Nazionale nonché centro d'interesse turistico e culturale. Per la sua importanza storica, la conservazione dei paesaggi esistenti è una norma urbanistica. La scelta, in questo caso, è stata quella di una versione semplificata della casa tradizionale a due piani con un garage a un'estremità.

Telluride é uma antiga localidade indígena e, posteriormente, acampamento mineiro, que actualmente é comarca Histórica Nacional e centro de interesse turístico e cultural. O seu carácter histórico fez com que a conservação das paisagens existentes seja uma norma urbanística. Assim, para esta casa, optou-se por uma versão simplificada da casa tradicional de dois andares com uma garagem numa extremidade.

Telluride är en gammal by som blev ett gruvsamhälle. Idag är det ett nationalhistoriskt område och en plats av kulturellt intresse och även populärt bland turister. På grund av dess historiska karaktär finns stadsutvecklingslagar som bevarar den existerande landsbygden, därför bestämdes det att en förenklad version av det traditionella tvåvåningshuset med garage i ena änden skulle byggas.

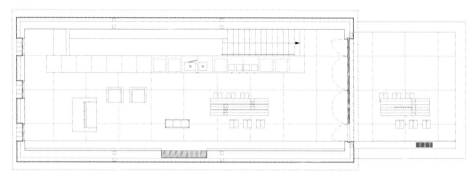

Second floor

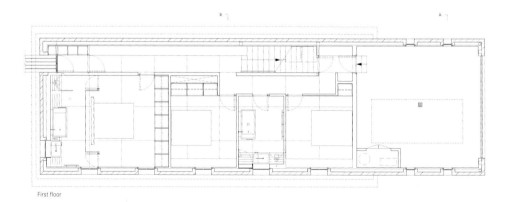

First floor

CASA DE **INGENIEROS**

SUSANA HERRERA/FACTORÍA DISEÑO Y CONSTRUCCIÓN
© José Luis Saavedra Morales

This house was built in the middle of a lush pine forest. The simple shapes of the property, its compact dimensions and the clever use of materials have meant it integrates with its surroundings. The walls show the characteristics of the concrete, which has been left exposed, and in some rooms only a coat of paint was added.

Cette maison a été bâtie au beau milieu d'une épaisse forêt de pins. La simplicité de ses formes, ses dimensions compactes et l'astucieux emploi des matériaux participent à sa parfaite intégration dans l'environnement. Les murs ont les caractéristiques du béton, laissé apparent ou recouvert d'une couche de peinture selon les pièces.

Dieses Haus befindet sich inmitten eines üppigen Pinienwaldes. Die einfachen Linien des Gebäudes, seine kompakten Ausmaße und der intelligente Einsatz der Materialien binden es hervorragend in die umliegende Landschaft ein. Die Mauern zeigen die für unverkleideten Beton typischen Eigenschaften, in manchen Räumen wurde er übermalt.

Dit huis staat midden in een naaldbomenbos. Door de simpele vormen, compacte afmetingen en het slimme materiaalgebruik gaat het huis volledig op in zijn omgeving. De wanden tonen de eigenschappen van het beton, dat onbedekt is gelaten. In sommige vertrekken is alleen een laag verf aangebracht.

Esta casa se levanta en medio de un exuberante bosque de pinos. Las formas simples del volumen, sus dimensiones compactas y el uso inteligente de los materiales permiten que se adapte al paisaje. Los muros muestran las características propias del hormigón, que no ha sido revestido, y en algunas habitaciones sólo recibió una capa de pintura.

Questa casa sorge nel mezzo di un esuberante bosco di pini. Le forme semplici del volume, le sue compatte dimensioni e l'uso intelligente dei materiali fanno sì che si adatti al paesaggio. I muri mostrano le caratteristiche proprie del cemento, che non è stato ricoperto, e in alcune stanze si è data solo una mano di pittura.

Esta casa ergue-se no meio de um exuberante bosque de pinheiros. As formas simples do volume, as dimensões compactas e a utilização inteligente dos materiais permitem que se adapte à paisagem. As paredes exibem as características típicas do betão, que não foi revestido e que em algumas divisões só recebeu uma demão de tinta.

Detta hus byggdes mitt i en frodig pinjeskog. Egendomens enkla former, dess kompakta dimensioner och den smarta användningen av material har gjort att den integreras med dess omgivningar. Väggarna, som har lämnats blottade, visar betongens egenskaper, i vissa rum har endast ett lager färg lagts till.

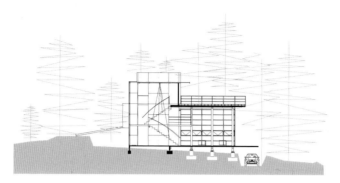

Section

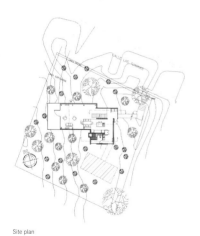

Site plan

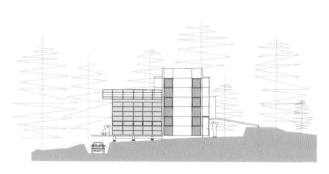

Elevation

ZEALANDIAHOUSE

Located in Portsea, Australia, this house was built in 1952. The architect felt that in renovating the property it was important to give the building a modern aspect which was linked to its history, and to maintain the 1950s style. A wide variety of materials were used for the walls of the property: paint, wood, stone and ceramic.

Cette maison de Portsea, en Australie, date de 1952. L'architecte chargé de la rénovation a voulu privilégier l'aspect moderne de l'édifice tout en lui conservant le style années 1950 qui fait partie de son histoire. Divers matériaux ont été employés dans l'habillage des murs, peinture, bois, pierre et céramique.

Dieses Haus befindet sich in Portsea (Australien) und wurde 1952 erbaut. Der Architekt wollte dem Gebäude im Zuge seiner Renovierung eine moderne Note verleihen, mit der an seine Geschichte angeschlossen und die Ästhetik der 50er Jahre erhalten werden sollte. Eine Vielfalt an Materialien kommt in seinem Inneren zum Einsatz: Farbe, Holz, Stein und Keramik.

Dit huis in Portsea, Australië, is gebouwd in 1952. De architect vond het belangrijk het pand bij de verbouwing een moderne uitstraling te geven en toch de stijl van de jaren vijftig te handhaven. Er zijn allerlei materialen gebruikt voor de wanden: verf, hout, steen en keramiek.

Situada en Portsea (Australia), esta casa se construyó en 1952. El arquitecto pensó que en la reforma era importante darle a la edificación un aspecto moderno, enlazando con su historia y manteniendo la estética de los años cincuenta. Multiplicidad de materiales conviven en las paredes de esta vivienda: pintura, madera, piedra y cerámica.

Sita a Portsea (Australia), questa casa fu edificata nel 1952. L'architetto ha pensato che nella ristrutturazione era importante dare all'edificio un aspetto moderno, pur senza perdere il contatto con la sua storia e conservando l'estetica degli anni cinquanta. Molteplici materiali convivono tra le pareti di questa casa: pittura, legno, pietra e ceramica.

Esta casa situada em Portsea (Austrália) foi construída em 1952. O arquitecto pensou que a reforma devia conferir-lhe um ar moderno, aproveitando a história da casa e mantendo a estética dos anos cinquenta. Nas paredes desta vivenda, encontramos os mais variados materiais: tinta, madeira, pedra e cerâmica.

Detta hus, beläget i Portsea i Australien, byggdes 1952. Arkitekten kände att det vid renoveringen var viktigt att ge byggnaden en modern känsla som var länkad till dess historia och att bevara 50talsstilen. Ett stort urval av material användes till väggarna på egendomen: färg, trä, sten och keramik.

Plan

BR HOUSE

MARCIO KOGAN
© Nelson Kor

This house was designed like an inverted terrarium and some of the rooms were completed with glass surrounds to afford views of the grove. The walls on the first floor are made from stone while those on the upper level are wooden. Both materials are indigenous to the region and enable the property to integrate with the surrounding countryside.

Cette maison a été conçue comme un terrarium inversé. Plusieurs pièces disposent de murs vitrés afin de donner vue sur le bois. Les murs du rez-de-chaussée sont en pierre et ceux de l'étage en bois. Il s'agit de matériaux locaux dont l'utilisation permet à la construction de se fondre dans le paysage.

Dieser Wohnraum wurde als "umgestülptes" Terrarium konzipiert, einige seiner Zimmer wurden mit Glastüren, die auf die Baumgruppe hinausgehen, verschlossen. Für die Mauern des unteren Stockwerks wurde Stein verwendet, im oberen Stock wurde mit Holz gearbeitet. Beide aus der Region stammenden Materialien binden das Haus optimal in die Landschaft ein.

Dit huis is ontworpen als een omgekeerd terrarium en sommige vertrekken zijn voorzien van glazen wanden om uitzicht op het bos te bieden. De wanden op de begane grond zijn van steen, die op de verdieping van hout. Beide materialen komen uit deze streek, waardoor de woning lijkt op te gaan in het landschap.

Esta vivienda se diseñó como un terrario invertido y algunas habitaciones fueron cerradas con puertas de cristal que se abren a la arboleda. Para los muros de la planta baja se utilizó la piedra mientras que la madera se reservó para la planta superior. Ambos materiales, provenientes de la región, permiten integrar la casa en el paisaje.

Questa casa è stata concepita come un terrario invertito e alcune stanze sono state chiuse mediante porte di vetro che si aprono sul bosco. Per i muri del pianterreno è stata impiegata la pietra mentre il legno è stato riservato per il piano superiore. Entrambi i materiali, provenienti dalla regione, fanno sì che la casa sia integrata nel paesaggio.

Esta vivienda foi desenhada como uma estufa invertida e alguns dos quartos foram fechados com portas de vidro que se abrem para o arvoredo. Para as paredes do rés-do-chão, usou-se pedra, reservando-se a madeira para o andar de cima. Ambos os materiais, provenientes da região, permitem integrar a casa na paisagem.

Detta hus designades som ett inverterat terrarium och en del av rummen kompletterades med omgivande glas för att få utsikt över lunden. Väggarna på första våningen är gjorda av sten medan de på det övre planet är av trä. Båda materialen är inhemska för området och möjliggör för fastigheten att smälta in i den omgivande landsbygden.

Site plan

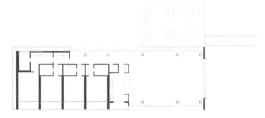

Plan

Elevation

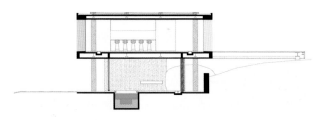

Section

00 HOUSE

FILIPPO BOMBACE
© Luigi Filetici

Very specific requests directed the focus of the renovation of this duplex, home to a family of four: to eliminate the hard corners of the structure, to avoid the use of industrial products and to keep the costs down. The two-colored flooring is based on the concepts of oriental Tao.

Les demandes précises formulées par les propriétaires de ce duplex où vit une famille de quatre personnes ont orienté toute la rénovation. Il fallait éliminer tous les angles saillants, éviter l'emploi de produits industriels et maintenir les coûts aussi bas que possible. Les sols de deux couleurs s'inspirent du concept du Tao.

Beim Umbau dieser Maisonnette-Wohnung, die eine vierköpfige Familie beherbergt, waren besonders spezifische Wünsche zu berücksichtigen: die Beseitigung von scharfen Ecken in der Struktur, die Vermeidung von Industrieprodukten, und die Einhaltung des Kostenvoranschlags. Der zweifarbige Boden entspricht dem orientalischen Tao-Prinzip.

Zeer specifieke verzoeken bepaalden de verbouwing van dit halfvrijstaande huis, waar een gezin van vier in woont: de scherpe hoeken van het pand wegnemen, een minimaal gebruik van industriële producten en de kosten laag houden. De tweekleurige vloer is gebaseerd op het yin-yang van het taoïsme.

Peticiones muy particulares caracterizaron el enfoque de la remodelación de este dúplex de una familia de cuatro personas: eliminar la presencia de cantos vivos en la estructura, evitar la adopción de productos industriales y contener el presupuesto de gastos. La pavimentación bicolor se basa en el concepto del Tao oriental.

L'approccio alla ristrutturazione di questo duplex di una famiglia di quattro persone è stato caratterizzato da alcune richieste molto particolari: eliminare la presenza di spigoli dalla struttura, evitare l'uso di prodotti industriali e contenere le spese. Il pavimento in due colori si basa sul concetto del Tao orientale.

A remodelação deste duplex de uma família de quatro pessoas respondeu a aspirações muito particulares: eliminar a presença de cantos vivos na estrutura, evitar a utilização de produtos industriais e reduzir o orçamento. A pavimentação bicolor baseia-se no conceito do Tao oriental.

Mycket specifika önskemål lade fokus på renoveringen av denna tvåvåningslägenhet, hem till en familj på fyra: att eliminera strukturens hårda hörn, undvika användning av industriella produkter och att hålla kostnaderna nere. Den tvåfärgade golvbeläggningen är baserad på tankarna i den orientaliska Tao.

VILLA **BIO**

Cloud 9 designed this house with large, sunny rooms which make the most of the natural light and afford views of the surroundings. The walls are made of concrete and glass. To increase the natural light large, triple glass sheets supported by a steel structure were installed.

Cloud 9, «le nuage neuf», est le nom de cette maison dont les pièces spacieuses et ensoleillées baignées par la lumière naturelle offrent de superbes panoramas sur les environs. Les murs associent verre et béton. Pour maximiser la lumière naturelle, des triples vitrages soutenus par une structure d'acier ont été posés.

Cloud 9 entwarf ein Haus mit geräumigen Zimmern mit reichlichem Sonneneinfall, um das natürliche Licht zu nutzen und einen freien Ausblick zu gewähren. Die Wände dieses Projekts sind aus Beton und Glas. Um den natürlichen Lichteinfall optimal zu nutzen, wurden große dreischichtige Glaslamellen verwendet, die von Stahlstrukturen getragen werden.

Dit huis is door Cloud 9 ontworpen met grote, zonnige vertrekken die het daglicht optimaal benutten en uitzicht op de omgeving bieden. De muren zijn van beton en glas. Om zoveel mogelijk daglicht toe te laten zijn er grote, driedubbele glasplaten in een stalen frame geplaatst.

Cloud 9 diseñó una vivienda con grandes habitaciones soleadas para aprovechar la luz natural y permitir una vista amplia hacia el exterior. Las paredes de este proyecto son de hormigón y cristal. Para ganar luminosidad natural se usaron grandes láminas de triple cristal sostenidas por estructuras de acero.

Cloud 9 ha progettato una casa caratterizzata da grandi stanze ben esposte al sole in modo da sfruttare al massimo la luce naturale e da permettere un'ampia vista all'esterno. Le pareti di questo progetto sono di cemento e vetro. Per avere una maggior luce naturale sono state impiegate grandi finestre di triplo vetro sostenute da strutture d'acciaio.

A Cloud 9 desenhou uma vivenda com grandes quartos solarengos para aproveitar a luz natural e permitir uma vista ampla para o exterior. As paredes deste projecto são de betão e vidro. Para ganhar luminosidade natural, recorreu-se a grandes placas de vidro triplo suportadas por estruturas de aço.

Cloud 9 designade detta hus med stora, soliga rum som gör det mesta av det naturliga ljuset och ger utsikt över omgivningarna. Väggarna är gjorda av betong och glas. För att öka det naturliga ljuset installerades stora treglasskivor, stöttade av ett stålskelett.

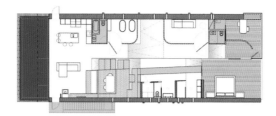

Plan

Elevation

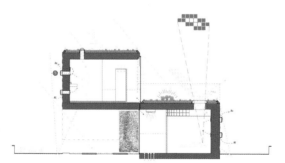

Transversal section

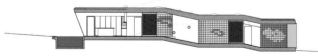

Longitudinal section

WILHELMINASTRAAT

HOFMAN DUJARDIN ARCHITECTEN
© Matthijs van Roon

This two-storey apartment is the result of a unique design: all the furnishing and decorative elements have been created exclusively for the property as requested by the client. The same materials, range of colors and details are repeated throughout the home.

Cet appartement en duplex est le résultat d'une conception unique puisque tout le mobilier et les éléments décoratifs ont été dessinés en même temps que les plans. Ce sont des pièces uniques réalisées à la demande du client. On retrouve dans toutes les pièces les mêmes matériaux, dans les mêmes gammes de couleurs et jusqu'au moindre détail.

Dieses aus zwei Stockwerken bestehende Appartement ist das Ergebnis eines einzigartigen Designs. Die gesamte Möblierung sowie alle dekorativen Elemente wurden speziell für diese Wohnung und nach den Wünschen des Kunden gefertigt. Die gleichen Materialien, Farbenspiele und Details finden sich in ihren verschiedenen Räumen wieder.

Dit drie verdiepingen tellende appartement is het resultaat van een uniek ontwerp: op verzoek van de cliënt zijn alle meubels en decoratieve elementen exclusief voor deze woning ontworpen. Alle materialen, kleuren en details komen steeds weer terug in het hele huis.

Este apartamento, compuesto por tres plantas, es producto de un diseño único: todo el mobiliario y los elementos decorativos han sido elaborados exclusivamente para el piso siguiendo los deseos del cliente. Los mismos materiales, las gamas de color y los detalles se repiten en los diferentes ambientes del hogar.

Questo appartamento, formato da due piani, è il risultato di un progetto unico: tutto l'arredamento e gli elementi decorativi sono stati realizzati in esclusiva seguendo le istruzioni del cliente. Gli stessi materiali, le gamme cromatiche e i particolari si susseguono ripetendosi nei vari ambienti.

Este apartamento, composto por dois andares, é produto de um design único: a totalidade do mobiliário e os elementos decorativos foram exclusivamente elaborados para o andar, respeitando a vontade do cliente. Os mesmos materiais, as gamas de cor e os pormenores repetem-se em todos os ambientes.

Denna tvåvåningslägenhet är resultatet av en unik design: alla möbler och dekorativa element har skapats exklusivt för egendomen på uppdrag av klienten. Samma material, färgnyanser och detaljer upprepas genom hela hemmet.

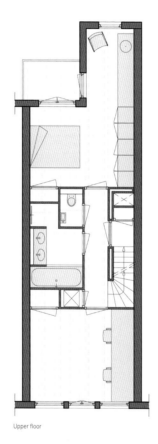

Upper floor

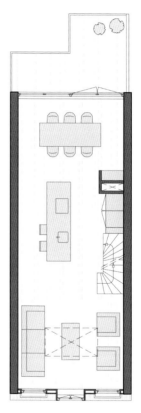

Lower floor

VILLA **SUND BJØRNSEN**

JARMUND-VIGNÆS ARKITEKTER
© Nils Petter Dale

Sund Bjørnsen is located between two hills on the small island of Nesøya in southern Norway. In order to integrate the property with its surroundings it has a staggered design, with wood being used as the main building material. The exterior structure is made of wood covered with copper, which reflects the sun in the most spectacular way.

Sund Bjørnsen est à deux collines de la petite île de Nesøya dans le sud de la Norvège. Le bâtiment s'élève sur plusieurs niveaux, ce qui lui permet de s'intégrer dans le paysage. Il est construit essentiellement en bois, même si la structure extérieure est recouverte de cuivre, afin que le soleil s'y reflète d'une manière spectaculaire.

Sund Bjørnsen liegt zwischen zwei Hügeln der kleinen Insel Nesøya, im Süden von Norwegen. Um es harmonisch in seine Umgebung einzubinden, wurde das Gebäude stufenförmig angelegt und Holz als Grundmaterial gewählt. Die Außenstruktur des Hauses ist aus mit Kupfer überzogenem Holz gefertigt, das das Sonnenlicht großartig reflektiert.

Sund Bjørnsen staat tussen twee heuvels op het eilandje Nesøya in het zuiden van Noorwegen. Om het huis te integreren in zijn omgeving is het verspringend van vorm gemaakt en is hout het voornaamste bouwmateriaal. De buitenkant is van hout bedekt met koper, dat de zon spectaculair weerkaatst.

Sund Bjørnsen está situada entre dos colinas en la pequeña isla de Nesøya, en el sur de Noruega. Para integrarlo armoniosamente al entorno, el edificio se diseñó con forma de escalera y se utilizó la madera como principal material de construcción. La estructura exterior de la casa está construida con madera revestida de cobre que refleja la luz solar de forma espectacular.

Sund Bjørnsen si trova tra due colline sulla piccola isola di Nesøya, al sud della Norvegia. Per integrare armonicamente l'edificio nel suo contesto, è stato progettato a forma di scala e come materiale edile è stato usato principalmente il legno. La struttura esterna della casa è stata costruita con legno ricoperto di rame che riflette in maniera spettacolare la luce solare.

Sund Bjørnsen fica situada entre duas colinas, na pequena ilha de Nesøya, no sul da Noruega. Para que ficasse harmoniosamente integrada no meio, a casa foi desenhada com a forma de uma escada e a madeira foi o material escolhido como tónica dominante da construção. A estrutura exterior da casa é construída em madeira revestida a cobre, que reflecte a luz solar de uma forma espectacular.

Sund Bjørnsen ligger mellan två kullar på den lilla ön Nesøya i södra Norge. För att integrera huset med dess omgivningar har det en ojämn design, med trä använt som det huvudsakliga byggnadsmaterialet. Den yttre strukturen är gjord av trä täckt med koppar som reflekterar solen på det mest spektakulära sätt.

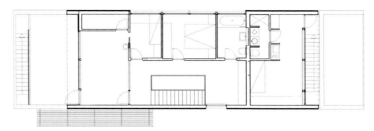

First floor

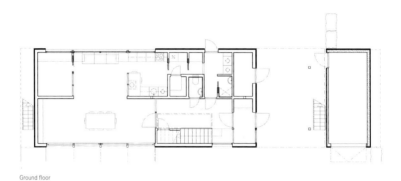

Ground floor

Cross section

Longitudinal section

VINEYARD ESTATE

Located at the bottom of a wooded mountain with extensive views over the vineyards and a valley, this monastic steel and stone structure is a private residence. The stone was chosen as the base material for the property as it is native to the area around the building.

Située au pied d'une montagne boisée et bénéficiant d'une superbe vue sur le vignoble, cette structure monastique toute de pierre et d'acier est une résidence privée. La pierre choisie comme matériau principal pour la construction est une roche locale.

Dieses klösterliche Gebilde aus Stein und Stahl befindet sich auf einem bewaldeten Berg und bietet einen Panoramablick über den Weingarten und das Tal. Es befindet sich in Privatbesitz. Der Stein wurde als Grundmaterial für dieses Haus gewählt, da er einen natürlichen Bestandteil der umliegenden Landschaft darstellt.

Dit imposante gebouw onder aan een beboste berg met een fraai uitzicht over de wijngaarden en een vallei is een privéwoning. Deze steensoort is gekozen als basismateriaal voor het huis, omdat deze voorkomt in het gebied rond de woning.

Situada en la base de una montaña arbolada, con vistas expansivas sobre una viña y un valle, esta estructura monacal de piedra y acero sirve como residencia privada. La piedra ha sido elegida como material base para esta vivienda por ser un componente de la geografía donde se emplaza la residencia.

Sita alla base di una montagna ricoperta d'alberi, con ampie viste su una vigna e su una valle, questa struttura monastica di pietra e acciaio funge da residenza privata. La pietra è stata scelta come materiale principale per questa casa in virtù del fatto che si tratta di un componente della zona geografica in cui sorge la residenza.

Situada no sopé de uma montanha arborizada com vistas amplas sobre uma vinha e um vale, esta estrutura monacal de pedra e aço serve de residência privada. Por ser um componente da natureza que envolve o edifício, a pedra foi o material escolhido para base desta vivenda.

Placerad vid foten av ett skogklätt berg med enorm utsikt över vingårdarna och en dal ligger denna klosterliknande stål- och stenkonstruktion som är ett privat hem. Stenen valdes som basmaterial till egendomen eftersom den finns naturligt i området runt byggnaden.

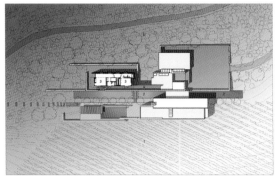

Upper floor

Elevation

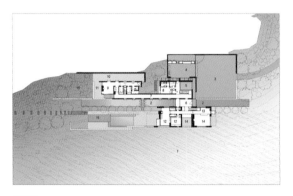

Mid floor

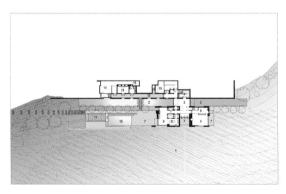

Lower floor

Sections

ROSA HOUSE

FILIPPO BOMBACE
© Luigi Filetici

The shapes in this elongated space proved a challenge for the designers during the renovation. With a limited budget and instructions to alter the original structure as little as possible, they chose colored drapes to interact in the space and create separations which were functional but at the same time expressive.

Les volumes de cet espace oblong ont mis les compétences des designers à rude épreuve. Avec un budget limité et la consigne de modifier aussi peu que possible la structure d'origine, ils ont opté pour des tapisseries colorées séparant les espaces. Cette interaction entre les panneaux textiles et l'espace s'avère aussi fonctionnelle qu'expressive.

Die Geometrie dieses länglichen Raums stellte für die Architekten eine Herausforderung bei der Renovierung dar. Sie hatten die Vorgabe, die Originalstruktur soweit wie möglich unverändert zu lassen und den knapp bemessenen Kostenrahmen einzuhalten. Sie entschieden sich dafür, starke Akzente mit kräftigen Farben zu setzen, um den Raum abwechslungsreich zu gestalten und funktionelle, ausdrucksstarke Trennungen zu schaffen.

De vormen in deze langwerpige ruimte vormden bij de verbouwing een uitdaging voor de ontwerpers. Met een beperkt budget en instructies om het oorspronkelijke bouwwerk zo min mogelijk te veranderen, kozen ze voor kleurige stoffen panelen die een wisselwerking met elkaar aangaan en afscheidingen creëren die functioneel, maar tegelijkertijd decoratief zijn.

Las geometrías en este espacio alargado fueron un desafío para los diseñadores en el momento de la renovación. Con un presupuesto ajustado y la consigna de alterar lo menos posible la estructura original, se recurrió a cortinados de colores para interactuar en el espacio y lograr separaciones funcionales a la vez que expresivas.

Le geometrie in questo spazio allungato, quando si è trattato di ristrutturare la casa, hanno rappresentato una grossa sfida per i progettisti. Con un budget limitato e l'ordine di alterare il meno possibile la struttura originale, si è fatto uso di tende colorate da far interagire nello spazio e ottenere separazioni funzionali oltre che espressive.

Neste espaço alongado, a geometria foi um verdadeiro desafio para os responsáveis pela renovação. Com um orçamento ajustado e a indicação de alterar o menos possível a estrutura original, optaram pelo recurso a cortinados de cores para interagirem no espaço e conseguirem separações funcionais e, simultaneamente, expressivas.

Formerna i detta avlånga utrymme visade sig vara en utmaning för designerna under renoveringen. Med en begränsad budget och instruktioner att ändra originalstrukturen så lite som möjligt, valde de att låta färgade draperier samspela i utrymmet och att skapa avskiljare som var funktionella men samtidigt uttrycksfulla.

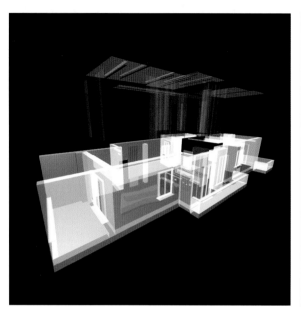

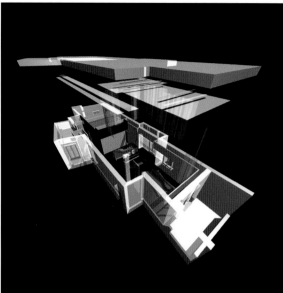

Render

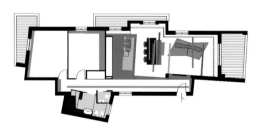

Plan

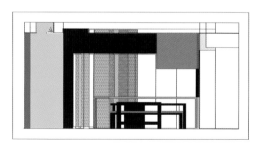

Section

BERGER HOUSE

JÜRG GRASER/GRASER ARCHITEKTEN
© Lilli Kel

This project stands out for its simple, clearly defined shapes. In order to make maximum use of the space for the garden, the house was raised perpendicularly to the slope and the first floor was shortened in such a way that the upper storey overhangs towards the garden.

La simplicité de ses formes clairement définies fait l'originalité de ce projet. Pour maximiser l'espace alloué au jardin, la maison a été surélevée perpendiculairement à la pente. Le rez-de-chaussée a été rétréci de sorte que l'étage avance en saillie sur le jardin.

Dieses Projekt sticht durch seine einfachen und klar definierten Formen hervor. Um soviel Raum wie möglich für den Garten nutzen zu können, wurde das Haus schräg an den Hang gebaut und der untere Stock zurückgesetzt, sodass der obere über den Garten hervorsteht.

Dit pand valt op door zijn eenvoudige, strakke vormen. Om de ruimte voor de tuin optimaal te benutten is het huis loodrecht op de helling geplaatst en is de begane grond zo ingekort dat de bovenverdieping boven de tuin uitsteekt.

Este proyecto destaca por las formas simples y claramente definidas. Con el fin de aprovechar al máximo el espacio para el jardín, se levantó la casa perpendicularmente a la pendiente y se retranqueó la planta baja, de manera que el piso superior sobresaliera hacia el jardín.

Questo progetto spicca per le sue forme semplici e chiaramente definite. Al fine di sfruttare al massimo lo spazio per il giardino, la casa è stata costruita perpendicolarmente alla pendenza e il pianterreno è stato fatto retrocedere, in modo tale che il piano superiore si sporga sul giardino.

Este projecto destaca-se pelas formas simples e claramente definidas. Com o objectivo de aproveitar ao máximo o espaço para o jardim, a casa foi edificada perpendicularmente em relação à encosta e o rés-do-chão recuado em relação ao andar de cima para que este se projectasse sobre o jardim.

Detta projekt sticker ut för dess enkla, tydligt definierade former. För att utnyttja utrymmet till trädgården maximalt restes huset lodrätt mot sluttningen och första våningen kortades på så sätt att den övre våningen hänger över mot trädgården.

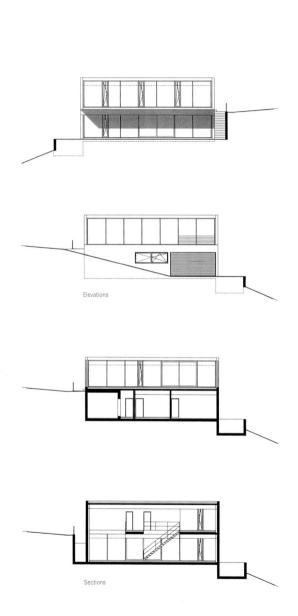

Elevations

Sections

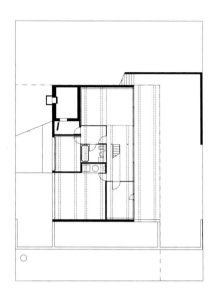

Ground floor

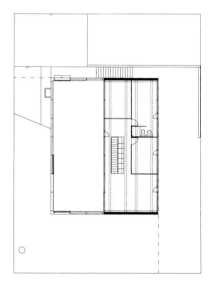

Basement

SECANO HOUSE

Located on dry terrain in Campo de Cartagena, the orientation of this house is north to south to protect it from the intense midday sun. Stones have been used to fill the exterior walls, and flat roofs with no slope, made from reinforced concrete, keep the interior of the house cool.

Sur un terrain sec, à Campo de Cartagena, cette maison est orientée nord-sud pour la protéger de la chaleur du soleil de midi. Les murs extérieurs doublés de pierres et le toit plat en béton armé contribuent à préserver la fraîcheur à l'intérieur.

Dieses Haus befindet sich auf einem trockenen Grundstück des Campo de Cartagena, und ist von Nord nach Süd ausgerichtet, um die intensive Mittagssonne zu vermeiden. Zur Auffüllung der Außenwände wurden Steine verwendet. Die flachen Dächer ermöglichen, eine angenehme Temperatur im Innenraum zu halten.

Dit huis staat op droog terrein in Campo de Cartagena. De as van het huis loopt van noord naar zuid om het te beschermen tegen de felle middagzon. Er zijn stenen gebruikt om de buitenmuren te vullen en platte daken van versterkt beton houden het huis vanbinnen koel.

Ubicada en un terreno secano del Campo de Cartagena, esta casa está orientada de norte a sur para resguardarla de la intensa luz solar del mediodía. Las piedras se utilizaron para rellenar las paredes exteriores. Techos planos y sin pendientes, realizados en concreto reforzado, permiten mantener el fresco en el interior del hogar.

Sita su un terreno non irrigato del Campo de Cartagena, questa casa è orientata da nord a sud per proteggersi dall'intensa luce solare del mezzogiorno. Le pietre sono state utilizzate per riempire le pareti esterne. Tetti piatti e privi di pendenze, costruiti in calcestruzzo rinforzato, permettono di conservare il fresco all'interno della casa.

Esta casa, situada num terreno de estiagem do Campo de Cartagena, tem orientação Norte para ficar resguardada da intensa luz solar do meio-dia. As pedras foram usadas para forrar as paredes exteriores. O telhado de betão armado, plano e sem inclinações permite manter o interior da casa sempre fresco.

Beläget i torr terräng i Campo de Cartagena är detta hus placerat mot norr till söder för att skydda det från den intensiva solen mitt på dagen. Stenar har använts för att fylla ytterväggarna och plana tak utan sluttning, gjorda av förstärkt betong, håller insidan av huset sval.

Plan

North elevation

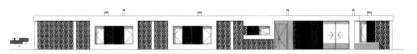

South elevation

West elevation

East elevation

BASSIL RESIDENCE

KAMAL HOMSI/ARCHIKA
© Geraldine Bruneel and Oussama Ayoub

This house was designed with leisure and relaxation in mind, so the surfaces are suitable for small groups of people, which met the client's requirements to be able to arrange parties and gatherings in the house. The flat roofs contrast with the eye-catching façades.

Tout dans les plans de cette maison visait à assurer la détente et le repos de ses occupants. Les surfaces sont destinées à recevoir de petits groupes de personnes, comme le souhaitait le client qui aime organiser des soirées intimes et des réunions chez lui. La sobriété des toits forme un contraste intéressant avec l'audace des façades.

Für das Design dieses Hauses war grundlegend, dass es dem Freizeitvergnügen und der Entspannung dienen sollte, daher wurden Bereiche geschaffen, in denen sich kleine Gruppen von Menschen bequem versammeln können, und die dem Wunsch des Kunden, in seinem Zuhause Feste und Treffen zu veranstalten, gerecht werden. Die flachen Dächer stehen im Kontrast zu den Fassaden, bei denen die ineinander greifenden Würfel hervorstechen.

Dit huis is ontworpen met vrije tijd en ontspanning in gedachten, dus zijn de oppervlakken geschikt voor kleine groepjes mensen, conform de wens van de cliënt om feestjes en bijeenkomsten in het huis te kunnen organiseren. De platte daken contrasteren met de opvallende gevelpartijen.

Esta casa se basa en las ideas de ocio y relajación, por lo que se crearon superficies adecuadas para reuniones de pequeños grupos de personas, que satisficieran el deseo del cliente de organizar fiestas y encuentros en su casa. La planicie de los techos contrasta con las fachadas resultantes del entrecruce de los cubos.

Questa casa si basa sui concetti di svago e relax, per tale ragione sono state adibite superfici adatte a riunioni di piccoli gruppi di persone, che soddisfano il desiderio del cliente di organizzare feste e ritrovi in casa sua. I tetti piatti creano un forte contrasto con le facciate ottenute dall'incrocio dei cubi.

A vontade do cliente de organizar festas e encontros em casa fez com que a ideia de ócio e descanso imperassem na concepção desta casa com superfícies adequadas para reuniões de pequenos grupos de pessoas. O telhado, muito plano, contrasta com as fachadas resultantes do encontro entre os cubos.

Detta hus designades med fritid och avkoppling i åtanke, så ytorna är lämpliga för små grupper av människor, vilket mötte klientens krav på att kunna arrangera partyn och sammankomster i huset. De plana yttertaken kontrasterar mot de iögonenfallande fasaderna.

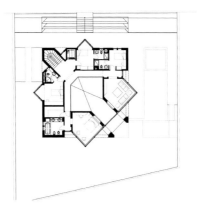

First floor

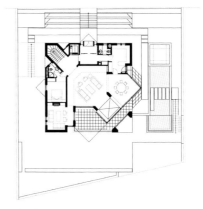

Ground floor

Basement

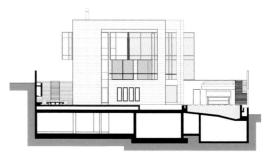

Section

GRAHAM AND LOUISE'S HOUSE

JEREMY HOADLEY
© Carlos Domínguez

This house has an architectural design with simple lines. Distributed over two storeys, both the levels and the spaces are well connected. The roof is sloped and covered in flat, black, Norman-style tiles.

Cette maison de deux étages se caractérise par la simplicité de son architecture. La circulation est aisée entre les pièces et d'un niveau à l'autre. Le toit à quatre pentes est recouvert de tuiles plates noires dans le style normand.

Dieses Einfamilienhaus gründet auf einem kargen architektonischen Design und einfachen Linien. Die beiden Stockwerke und die Räume sind optimal miteinander verbunden. Die Außenseite seines Schrägdachs wurde mit flachen schwarzen Ziegel im normannischen Stil verkleidet.

Dit huis heeft een fraai ontwerp met simpele lijnen. Het is verdeeld over twee verdiepingen en zowel de twee woonlagen als de vertrekken onderling zijn goed met elkaar verbonden. Het dak loopt schuin af en is bedekt met platte, zwarte tegels.

Esta vivienda unifamiliar presenta un diseño arquitectónico austero y de líneas simples. Dividida en dos niveles, tanto las plantas como los ambientes se encuentran muy bien comunicados entre sí. La techumbre de esta casa ha sido construida en pendiente y está revestida por el exterior con tejas planas de color negras de tipo normandas.

Questa casa unifamiliare presenta un progetto architettonico austero e dalle linee semplici. È divisa su due livelli e tanto i piani quanto gli ambienti sono perfettamente comunicanti tra loro. Il tetto di questa casa è stato realizzato in pendenza ed è ricoperto all'esterno con tegole piane di colore nero del tipo che si trova in Normandia.

Esta vivenda unifamiliar exibe um design arquitectónico austero e de linhas simples. Está dividida em dois níveis muito bem comunicados entre si, o mesmo sucedendo no que aos ambientes diz respeito. O telhado desta casa foi construído com inclinação e revestido com telhas planas e pretas, de tipo normandas.

Detta hus har en arkitektonisk design med enkla linjer. Det är fördelat över två våningar där båda planen och utrymmena är väl förenade. Yttertaket är sluttande och täckt med plana, svarta plattor i normandstil.

House axonometry

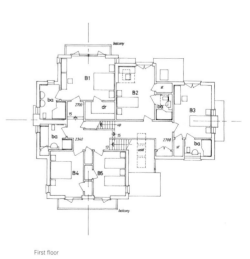

First floor

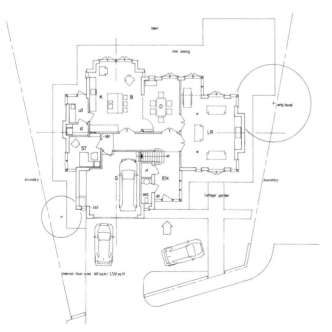

Ground floor

VALLDOREIX RESIDENCE

UJO PALLARÉS / ARS SPATIUM
© Jordi Miralles

The client wanted a house with simple lines, and special priority given to the relation with the exterior and to the interior communication. The design was drawn up around a wall which runs parallel to the street. The roofs are concrete, flat and without slopes. The staggered form of the exterior is repeated on the ceiling inside.

Le client voulait une demeure aux lignes épurées. La priorité était de privilégier le lien avec l'extérieur, tout en apportant le plus grand soin à la communication entre les volumes intérieurs. Le plan s'organise autour d'un mur central parallèle à la route. Les toits terrasses sont en béton. Le profil découpé de l'extérieur se retrouve à l'intérieur au niveau des plafonds.

Der Kunde wünschte sich karge Linien und eine besondere Betonung des Zusammenspiels zwischen Außen- und Innenraum sowie der Verbindung der Innenräume. Der Entwurf setzt an einer parallel zur Straße verlaufenden Mauer an. Die Dächer sind aus Beton, flach und ohne Gefälle. Die stufenartigen Formen des Äußeren wurden auch an der Dachinnenseite weitergeführt.

De klant wilde een huis met simpele lijnen en aandacht voor de relatie met de omgeving. Het ontwerp is gemaakt rond een muur die evenwijdig aan de straat loopt. De daken zijn van beton, plat en zonder hellende vlakken. De verspringende vorm van de omgeving wordt binnen herhaald op het plafond.

El cliente planteó una casa de formas austeras con una prioridad especial a la relación con el exterior y a la comunicación interior. Se articuló el diseño alrededor de un muro que corre paralelo a la calle. Los techos son de hormigón, planos y sin pendientes. Las formas escalonadas del exterior también se aplicaron en la techumbre del interior.

Il cliente ha voluto una casa dalle forme austere con una particolare importanza concessa al rapporto con l'esterno e alla comunicazione interna. Il progetto è stato dunque articolato intorno a un muro che corre parallelo alla via esterna. I tetti sono di cemento, piatti e senza pendenze. Le forme scalate degli esterni sono state applicate anche alla tettoia dell'interno.

O cliente pensou numa casa com formas austeras e que privilegiasse a relação com o exterior e a comunicação com o interior. Assim, a casa foi concebida em articulação com um muro que corre ao longo da rua. Os telhados são de betão, planos e sem inclinação. As formas escalonadas do exterior também foram aplicadas na parte interna do telhado.

Klienten ville ha ett hus med enkla linjer och särskild prioritet gavs till relationen mellan utom- och inomhuskommunikationen. Designen ritades utifrån en vägg som löper parallellt med gatan. Yttertaken är i betong, platta och utan sluttningar. Exteriörens ojämna form upprepas i innertaket.

Elevations

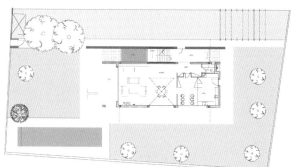

Ground floor

First floor

PORTAS NOVAS HOUSE

VÍCTOR CAÑAS
© Jordi Miralle

The house is located on the Guanacaste peninsula in northern Costa Rica, and is totally adapted to the terrain. Inside, the absence of color and the basic furnishings enable the tones of the exterior to penetrate the house. Glass and cement are the materials which are most evident in the construction.

Cette demeure se trouve sur l'île de Guanacaste dans le nord du Costa Rica. Elle est parfaitement adaptée à son environnement. À l'intérieur, l'absence de toute couleur et le minimalisme du mobilier permettent de s'imprégner des tonalités de l'extérieur. Le verre et le ciment sont les matériaux les plus présents dans cette construction.

Das Projekt befindet sich nördlich von Costa Rica auf der Guanacaste-Insel und ist perfekt in die landschaftliche Topografie eingebunden. Der Innenraum ist farblos und seine Möblierung einfach gehalten, wodurch die Farben aus dem Äußeren in den Innenraum dringen können. Bei dieser Konstruktion wurde hauptsächlich mit Glas und Zement gearbeitet.

Dit huis bevindt zich op het schiereiland Guanacaste in het noorden van Costa Rica en is volledig aangepast aan het terrein. Binnen zorgen de afwezigheid van kleur en de eenvoudige meubels ervoor dat de tinten van buiten binnen worden voortgezet. Glas en cement zijn de meest zichtbare bouwmaterialen.

La vivienda se encuentra en la península de Guanacaste, en el norte de Costa Rica, y está totalmente adaptada a la topografía del terreno. En el interior, la ausencia de color y el mobiliario básico permiten que las tonalidades del exterior penetren en la casa. El vidrio y el cemento son los materiales que más destacan en esta construcción.

La casa si trova sulla penisola di Guanacaste, nella zona settentrionale del Costa Rica ed è completamente adattata alla topografia del terreno. All'interno, l'assenza di colore e l'arredamento ridotto ai minimi termini fanno si che i toni dell'esterno penetrino in casa. Il vetro e il cemento sono i materiali che spiccano maggiormente.

A vivenda encontra-se na península de Guanacaste, no norte da Costa Rica, e foi totalmente adaptada à topografia do terreno. No interior, a ausência de cor e o mobiliário clássico permitem que as tonalidades do exterior penetrem na casa. O vidro e o cimento são os materiais que mais se destacam nesta construção.

Huset är beläget på Guanacastehalvön i norra Costa Rica, och är helt anpassat till terrängen. På insidan möjliggör frånvaron av färg och den grundläggande möbleringen tonerna från exteriören att ta sig in i huset. Glas och cement är de material som är mest uppenbara i konstruktionen.

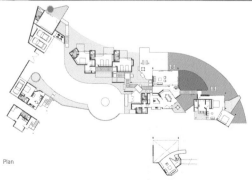

Plan

SHIMOSAKUNOBE K

RICO TURU ARCHITECTS
© Shin Fhoto Work

Located on top of a hill, this house – which is also a small office – was designed as a look-out point. With the spectacular views in mind, the spaces were arranged so that the surroundings could be enjoyed from different perspectives.

Au sommet d'une colline, cette maison, qui est aussi un petit bureau, fut conçue comme un belvédère. Le panorama spectaculaire a guidé l'architecte qui a distribué les espaces, de sorte que l'on puisse apprécier la vue depuis des perspectives différentes.

Dieses auf dem Gipfel eines Hügels stehende Haus, das gleichzeitig als kleines Büro dient, wurde als Aussichtwarte geplant. Unter Berücksichtigung des herrlichen Panoramas, wurden die Räume so entworfen, dass sie verschiedene Perspektiven auf die umliegende Natur gewähren.

Dit huis, waarin ook een klein kantoor is ondergebracht, staat boven op een heuvel en is ontworpen als uitkijkpunt. Met de spectaculaire uitzichten in gedachten zijn de ruimtes zo gerangschikt dat de omgeving vanuit verschillende perspectieven kan worden bekeken.

Situada en lo alto de una colina, esta vivienda, que también funciona como una pequeña oficina, se concibió como si fuera un mirador. Considerando las vistas privilegiadas, se diseñaron los espacios de forma que se pudiera apreciar la naturaleza desde perspectivas diferentes.

Sita sulla cima di una collina, quest'abitazione, che funge anche da piccolo ufficio, è stata concepita come se fosse un belvedere. Considerando le viste privilegiate che si godono, gli spazi sono stati disegnati in modo tale da poter apprezzare la natura da punti di vista differenti.

Além de também funcionar como escritório, esta casa de habitação situada no alto de uma colina foi concebida como se fosse um miradouro. Tendo como elemento primordial a espectacularidade da vista, os espaços foram planificados de forma a permitirem apreciar a natureza de perspectivas diferentes.

Detta hus, - som även är ett litet kontor - beläget på toppen av en kulle designades som en utsiktspunkt. Med den spektakulära utsikten i åtanke arrangerades utrymmena så att omgivningarna kunde njutas av ur olika perspektiv.

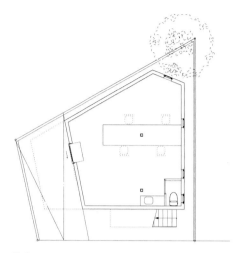

First floor

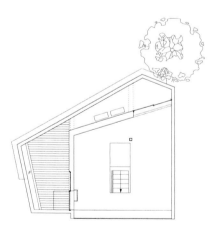

Second floor

Third floor

Fourth floor

TOMATENSTRAAT

HOFMAN DUJARDIN ARCHITECTEN
© Matthijs van Roon

The living room, dining room, kitchen and bedrooms all open onto a garden which runs the length of one side of the property. The whole house receives plenty of natural light through its numerous windows, turning it into a transparent space linked to the natural surroundings.

Salon, salle à manger, cuisine et chambres ouvrent sur le jardin qui borde un côté de la maison. L'éclairage naturel est abondant grâce aux nombreuses fenêtres. Il fait de cette demeure un espace transparent en symbiose avec son environnement.

Das Wohnzimmer, das Esszimmer, die Küche und die Schlafzimmer sind über einen über die Längsseite des Grundstücks verlaufenden Garten miteinander verbunden. Der großzügige Lichteinfall im gesamten Gebäude wird durch seine zahlreichen Öffnungen erreicht und wandelt es in ein transparentes, mit der Natur verbundenes Gebilde.

De woonkamer, eetkamer, keuken en slaapkamers komen allemaal uit op een tuin die over de hele lengte opzij van de woning loopt. Het hele huis krijgt volop daglicht door de vele ramen, waardoor het een transparant geheel wordt dat in verbinding staat met zijn natuurlijke omgeving.

La sala de estar, el comedor, la cocina y los dormitorios se encuentran conectados a través de un jardín que se extiende a lo largo de uno de los lados de la propiedad. La generosa cantidad de luz que recibe toda la vivienda, gracias a la profusión de aberturas, la transforma un espacio transparente y vinculado a la naturaleza.

Il soggiorno, la sala da pranzo, la cucina e le camere da letto sono uniti mediante un giardino disposto parallelamente rispetto a uno dei lati della proprietà. L'abbondante quantità di luce che riceve tutta la casa, grazie all'elevato numero di aperture, la converte in uno spazio trasparente e a contatto con la natura.

A sala de estar e a de jantar, a cozinha e os quartos estão ligados através de um jardim que se estende ao longo de um dos lados da propriedade. A grande quantidade de luz que toda a vivenda recebe graças à profusão de aberturas, faz com que seja um espaço transparente e em estreita união com a natureza.

Vardagsrummet, matrummet, köket och sovrummen är alla öppna mot en trädgård som löper längs med en sida av fastigheten. Hela huset får massor av naturligt ljus genom dess många fönster, som förvandlar det till ett genomskinligt utrymme länkat till de naturliga omgivningarna.

AIGUABLAVA

JOSEP MARIA FONT/GREEK DESIGN
© Joan Mund

The Costa Brava is characterized by a rocky landscape, small coves, and cliffs, which enable the construction of houses with views of the sea. Aiguablava is the result of the renovation of an existing house, and although the original had no views of the sea, the huge windows in the new property mean that the interior merges with the spectacular Mediterranean coastline.

La Costa Brava est connue pour ses côtes rocheuses, ses anses sablonneuses et ses falaises surmontées de maisons avec vue imprenable sur la Méditerranée. Avant sa rénovation, cette demeure ne disposait pas d'ouverture sur la mer. Aujourd'hui, grâce aux immenses baies vitrées, l'intérieur se fond dans le bleu spectaculaire des eaux marines.

Die Costa Brava zeichnet sich durch eine steinige Landschaft mit zahlreichen Buchten und Klippen aus, die sich für den Bau von Häusern mit Meeresblick anbietet. Aiguablava ist das Resultat einer Renovierung, die an einem bereits vorhandenen Haus ohne Meeresausblick vorgenommen wurde. Die großen Glasfenster lassen das Innere des Hauses mit der umliegenden mediterranen Landschaft verschmelzen.

De Costa Brava wordt gekenmerkt door een rotsachtig landschap, kleine inhammen en klippen, waardoor er huizen met uitzicht op zee kunnen worden gebouwd. Aiguablava had geen uitzicht op zee, maar na de verbouwing lijkt het interieur in verbinding te staan met de spectaculaire mediterrane kust door de enorme ramen.

La Costa Brava se caracteriza por un paisaje rocoso, de pequeñas calas y acantilados, que permite construir casas con vistas al mar. Aiguablava es el resultado de la renovación de una casa preexistente que carecía de ellas. Los grandes ventanales de cristal permiten fundir el interior de la vivienda con el espectacular paisaje mediterráneo.

La Costa Brava è caratterizzata da un paesaggio roccioso, costellato da calette e scogliere, in cui è possibile costruire case con viste sul mare. Aiguablava è il risultato della ristrutturazione di una casa che aveva un gran bisogno di riforme. Grazie ai finestroni di vetro è possibile fondere l'interno dell'abitazione con lo spettacolare paesaggio mediterraneo.

A Costa Brava caracteriza-se por ter uma paisagem rochosa, com pequenas baías e falésias, que permitem construir casas com vista para o mar. Aiguablava é o resultado da renovação de uma casa preexistente, que não tirava partido da vista. As grandes janelas de vidro permitem fundir o interior da vivenda com a espectacular paisagem mediterrânica.

Costa Brava karaktäriseras av ett stenigt landskap, små vikar och klippor, vilket möjliggör huskonstruktioner med havsutsikt. Aiguablava är resultatet av renovering av ett existerande hus och trots att originalet inte hade havsutsikt innebär den nya fastighetens enorma fönster att interiören blandar sig med den spektakulära medelhavskusten.

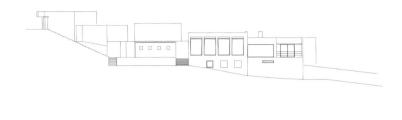

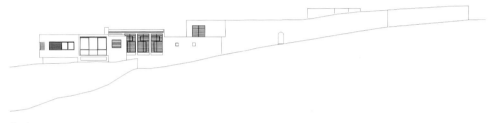

Elevations

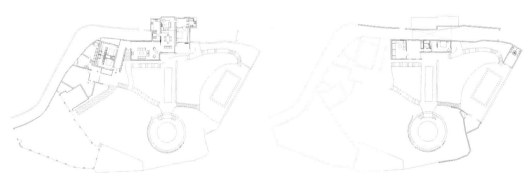

Ground floor

Basement

ANTÓN 10

WOLFGANG PÖSCHL, DIETOR COMPLOJ/TATANKA IDEENVERTRIEBSGESELLSCHAFT
© Toni Leichner

In accordance with the strict laws in the region which prohibit the construction of roof terraces, this house was designed on three storeys, resulting in the surprising effect of a classical temple. The glass is reflective in order to create privacy inside and to protect the interior from the high mountain sun.

La réglementation locale très stricte interdisant les toits en terrasse, cet édifice de deux étages prend des airs de temple classique. Le verre réfléchissant préserve l'intimité de l'intérieur tout en le protégeant de la forte réverbération du soleil en haute montagne.

Den strengen Gesetzen der Region entsprechend, die den Bau von Flachdächern untersagen, wurde ein dreistöckiges Gebäude errichtet. Das Gebäude beeindruckt durch seine Ähnlichkeit mit einem klassischen Tempel. Die Gläser besitzen einen hohen Reflektionsgrad, um die Intimsphäre der Bewohner zu gewährleisten und sie vor den Gebirgssonnenstrahlen zu schützen.

Overeenkomstig de strenge wetten in dit gebied die de bouw van dakterrassen verbieden, is dit huis met drie verdiepingen ontworpen als een soort klassieke tempel. Het glas is reflectief om redenen van privacy en om bescherming tegen de hoge bergzon te bieden.

De acuerdo con las estrictas leyes de la región, que no permiten la construcción de azoteas, se diseñó una vivienda de tres pisos. El edificio resulta sorprendente, debido a su parecido con un templo clásico. Los cristales tienen un alto grado de reflexión para preservar la intimidad y protegerla de los rayos solares de la alta montaña.

Nel rispetto delle dure leggi della regione, che non permettono la costruzione di terrazze, è stata progettata una casa di tre piani. L'edificio risulta sorprendente, a causa della sua somiglianza con un tempio classico. I vetri presentano un elevato grado di riflessione per preservare l'intimità e proteggerla dai raggi solari dell'alta montagna.

Respeitando as leis restritas da região, que não permitem a construção de terraços, desenhou-se uma vivenda com três andares. O edifício é surpreendente, devido à sua semelhança com um templo clássico. Os vidros têm um grau de reflexão elevado para permitir preservar a intimidade e protegê-la dos raios solares da montanha.

I enlighet med de strikta lagar i området som förbjuder konstruktion av takterrasser, designades detta hus i tre våningar, vilket resulterade i en överraskande effekt av ett klassiskt tempel. Glaset reflekterande för att skapa avskildhet inomhus och för att skydda interiören från den höga solen i bergen.

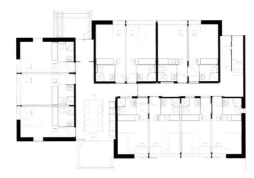

First floor

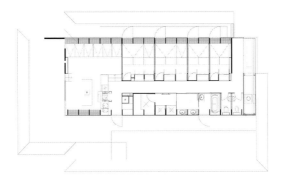

Ground floor

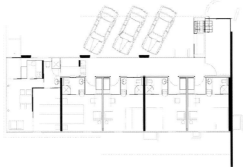

Basement

TREE HOUSE

VAN DER MERWE MISZEWSKI ARCHITECTS
© Van der Merwe Miszewski Architects

The iconic trees of Africa and the pine forest setting provided the reference for the design of this building. Five "trees" serve as the anchoring structures from the ground to the roof, which comprises a wooden box and a light flagstone, and has deliberately been separated from the perimeter.

Les arbres emblématiques de l'Afrique et la pinède environnante ont inspiré les plans de l'édifice. Cinq «arbres» ancrent la structure depuis le sol jusqu'à la toiture. Côté plafond, on remarque les caissons en bois sur lesquels repose une dalle minérale légère, délibérément surélevée au-dessus du périmètre.

Bezugspunkt für die Struktur des Gebäudes waren die ikonenhaften afrikanischen Bäume und der umliegende Pinienwald. Das Dach ist über eine aus fünf Bäumen bestehende Struktur mit dem Boden verankert. Das aus einer Holzstruktur und einer leichtgewichtigen Platte bestehende Dach wurde absichtlich vorn über die Außenkante hinaus gebaut.

De iconische bomen van Afrika en het naaldbos op de achtergrond vormden het uitgangspunt voor het ontwerp van dit huis. Vijf "bomen" dragen het houten dak, dat bewust gescheiden is van het stalen geraamte.

La iconicidad de los árboles en África y el entorno del pinar proporcionaron la referencia para decidir la estructura del edificio. Cinco árboles funcionan como estructuras de anclaje del techo hacia el suelo. El techo, compuesto por una caja de madera y una losa ligera, se ha separado deliberadamente del borde perimetral.

Il carattere iconico degli alberi in Africa e il contesto della pineta hanno dato l'idea per delineare la struttura dell'edificio. Cinque alberi funzionano come sistemi d'ancoraggio del tetto al suolo. Il soffitto, formato da cassettoni di legno e lastre leggere, è stato deliberatamente separato dal bordo perimetrale.

A representação das árvores africanas e a proximidade do pinhal condicionaram a escolha da estrutura do edifício. Cinco «árvores» funcionam como estrutura de apoio do telhado até ao chão. O telhado, formado por uma caixa de madeira e uma placa de pedra leve, foi deliberadamente separado dos limites do perímetro.

Afrikas symboliska träd och inramningen av pinjeskogen bidrog med referenserna till designen av denna byggnad. Fem "träd" tjänar som förankrande strukturer från marken till taket, som består av en trälåda och en lätt stenplatta och har medvetet separerats från omgivningen.

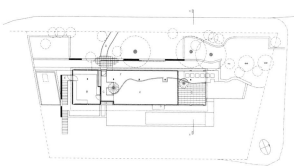

Second floor

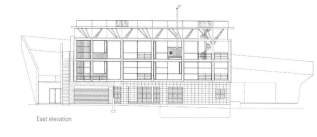

East elevation

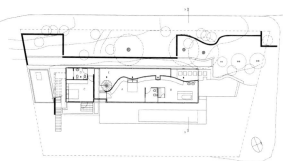

First floor

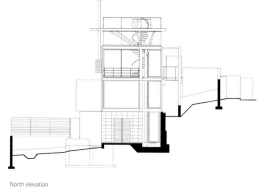

North elevation

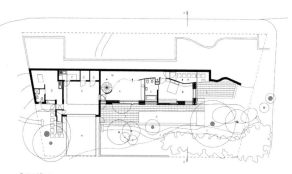

Ground floor

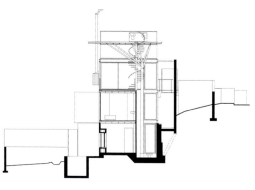

Cross section

TOORAK HOUSE

B. E. ARCHITECTURE
© Shania Shegedyr

As the lot is surrounded by single-storey houses, this property was closed on the side which gives onto the street in order to create a large interior courtyard, which houses the entrance. The open design, and the fact that many of the walls have large openings, mean that the rooms all receive plenty of light and a refreshing breeze.

Le terrain étant entouré de maisons de plain-pied, la façade côté rue a été fermée afin d'agrandir le vaste patio intérieur qui fait fonction d'entrée. Le plan très aéré et les larges ouvertures des murs font que toutes les pièces sont lumineuses et bénéficient d'une brise rafraîchissante.

Da das Grundstück von einstöckigen Einfamilienhäusern umgeben ist, wurde es straßenseitig geschlossen, um einen großen Innenhof zu schaffen, der als Vorraum dient. Dank des offenen Designs und der Wände, die Innen- und Außenraum eher verbinden als trennen, werden die Räume mit ausreichend Licht und einer kühlen Brise versorgt.

Omdat de kavel omringd is door woningen met één verdieping is dit huis aan de straatzijde afgesloten om een grote binnenplaats te creëren waar de entree zich bevindt. Door het open ontwerp en de grote openingen in de wanden krijgen alle vertrekken volop licht en frisse lucht.

Puesto que el terreno está rodeado por viviendas unifamiliares de una planta, la casa se cerró por el lado de la calle para crear un gran patio interior, donde se colocó el vestíbulo. Gracias al diseño abierto -y a que muchas de las paredes son más bien grandes aberturas-, las habitaciones reciben la luz adecuada y una brisa refrescante.

Dal momento che il terreno è circondato da abitazioni unifamiliari di un solo piano, la casa è stata chiusa dalla parte che dà sulla via per creare un grande cortile interno, in cui è stato posto il vestibolo. Grazie al progetto aperto -e al fatto che molte pareti sono in realtà grandi aperture-, le stanze ricevono la quantità di luce necessaria e una rinfrescante brezza.

Considerando que o terreno está rodeado de vivendas unifamiliares térreas, a casa foi fechada pelo lado que dá para a rua e criou-se um pátio interior onde se colocou a entrada. Graças ao desenho aberto — e ao facto de muitas paredes serem grandes aberturas —, os aposentos recebem a quantidade de luz adequada e uma brisa refrescante.

Eftersom tomten är omgiven av enplanshus slöts fastigheten på den sida som vetter mot gatan för att skapa en stor innergård som hyser entrén. Den öppna designen och det faktum att många av väggarna har stora öppningar betyder att alla rum får mycket ljus och en uppfriskande vind.

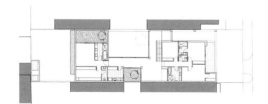

Ground floor

First floor

LORES HOUSE

JOAN JESÚS PUIG DE AYGUAVIVES, CLAUDIA RUEDA VELÁZQUE
© Jordi Miralle

Surrounded by olive, carob and palm trees indigenous to the region, this urban house has a wenge wood staircase as its central element, connecting the different levels. Sliding doors have been used to make spaces larger, as seen between the living and dining rooms, and in the room adjoining the master bedroom.

Entourée d'oliviers, de caroubiers et de palmiers indigènes de la région, cette maison de ville est remarquable pour son escalier en wengé, élément central qui relie tous les niveaux. Les portes coulissantes agrandissent encore l'espace entre le salon et la salle à manger, ainsi qu'entre la grande chambre et la pièce voisine.

Von Olivenbäumen, Johannisbrotbäumen und den für die Region typischen Palmen umgeben, steht im Mittelpunkt dieses städtischen Einfamilienhauses eine Stiege aus Wengé, die die verschiedenen Stockwerke miteinander verbindet. Zur Erweiterung der Räumlichkeiten wurden Schiebetüren eingesetzt, so zum Beispiel im Wohnzimmer, im Esszimmer und in dem an das Hauptschlafzimmer anschließenden Raum.

Dit stadshuis wordt omringd door de in dit gebied veelvoorkomende olijf-, carob- en palmbomen. Een trap van wengéhout vormt het centrale element, dat de woonlagen met elkaar verbindt. Schuifdeuren vergroten de ruimtes, bijvoorbeeld tussen de woon- en eetkamer en in het vertrek naast de ouderslaapkamer.

Rodeada de olivos, algarrobos y palmeras típicas de la región, esta casa unifamiliar urbana tiene como elemento central una escalera hecha de madera de wengué, que conecta las distintas plantas. Se han utilizado puertas correderas para ampliar ambientes, como es el caso del salón y el comedor, y de la sala contigua al dormitorio principal.

Circondata da olivi, carrubi e palme tipiche della regione, questa casa unifamiliare urbana possied come elemento centrale una scala di legno di wengè, che mette in comunicazione i vari piani. Son state utilizzate porte scorrevoli per ampliare ambienti, per esempio nel soggiorno e nella sala da pranzo, nonché nella sala contigua alla camera da letto principale.

Rodeada de oliveiras, alfarrobeiras e palmeiras típicas da região, esta casa unifamiliar urbana te como elemento central uma escada feita de madeira de wengué que dá acessibilidade aos vári andares. Foram usadas portas de correr para ampliar ambientes, como no caso da sala de estar de jantar, e da sala contigua ao quarto principal.

Omgivet av olivträd, karob och palmer som är inhemska för regionen, har detta hus i staden en trappa av wengeträ som sitt centrala element som förbinder de olika planen. Skjutdörrar har använts för att göra utrymmen större, vilket kan ses mellan vardags- och matrummen, och i rummet som ligger intill huvudsovrummet.

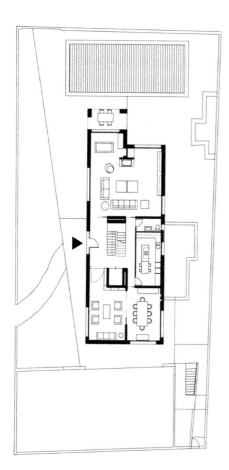

Ground floor

First floor

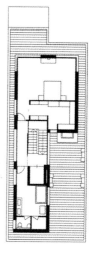

Second floor

LOSA LOFT

The young married couple who own this property wanted to transform it into a designer loft. Located in San Francisco's Mission District, the house was converted to create a very functional space made up of simple details in keeping with the couple's urban life style.

Le jeune couple propriétaire du lieu voulait en faire un «designer loft». Située dans le Mission District à San Francisco, la maison a été entièrement refaite pour devenir un espace des plus fonctionnels, parfaitement adapté au mode de vie urbain de ses habitants.

Die Besitzer dieses Hauses, ein junges Ehepaar, wollten dieses zu einem *Loft* umgestalten. Das Haus befindet sich im Mission District in San Francisco und wurde in einen sehr funktionellen Raum umgestaltet, dessen einfache Details den urbanen Lebensstil des Paars widerspiegeln.

Het jonge echtpaar aan wie dit pand toebehoort, wilde het verbouwen tot een designloft. Het huis, dat in het Mission District in San Francisco staat, werd verbouwd tot een zeer functionele ruimte met allerlei simpele details die passen bij de stedelijke leefstijl van de bewoners.

Los dueños de esta vivienda, un joven matrimonio, deseaban transformarla en un *loft* de diseño. Situado en el Mission District de San Francisco, la casa se convirtió en un espacio muy funcional, compuesto por sencillos detalles en consonancia con el estilo de vida urbano de la pareja.

I proprietari di questa casa, una giovane coppia, volevano trasformarla in un *loft* di design. Sita nel Mission District di San Francisco, l'abitazione è divenuta uno spazio molto funzionale, formato da semplici dettagli in consonanza con lo stile di vita urbano della coppia.

Os proprietários desta vivenda, um casal jovem, pretendiam transformá-la num *loft* de design. Situada no Mission District de São Francisco, a casa tornou-se um espaço muito funcional, composto por pormenores simples em harmonia com o estilo de vida urbano do casal.

Det unga gifta paret som äger denna fastighet ville förvandla det till ett designerloft. Huset, beläget i San Franciscos Mission District, omvandlades för att skapa ett mycket funktionellt utrymme gjort av enkla detaljer som stämmer med parets urbana livsstil.

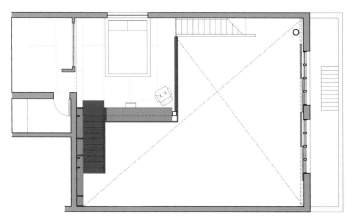

Mezzanine

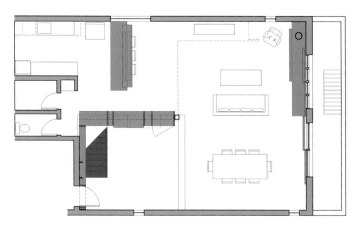

Ground floor

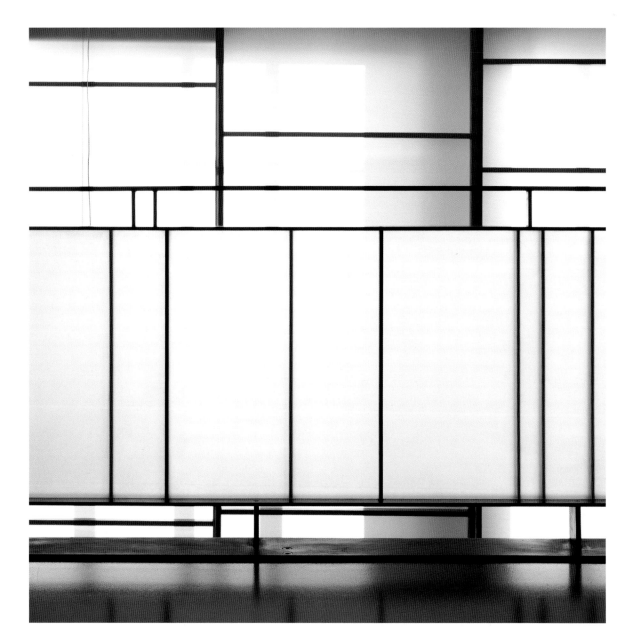

PLANTAGE KERKLAAN

HOFMAN DUJARDIN ARCHITECTEN
© Matthijs van Roor

This apartment in Amsterdam is interesting for the visual continuity of the spaces. Even an area as private as the bathroom is open to the other rooms. The color white is predominant throughout the property, with pale oak veneer to increase the feeling of light.

La continuité visuelle des espaces de cet appartement d'Amsterdam retient l'attention. Même une pièce aussi intime que la salle de bains est ouverte sur les autres. Le blanc prédomine, relevé par un vernis chêne pâle qui accentue la luminosité.

Dieses Appartement befindet sich im Süden von Amsterdam, an seinen Räumen ist bemerkenswert, dass sie ineinander zu fließen scheinen. Sogar ein so privater Raum wie das Bad ist den restlichen Räumlichkeiten gegenüber offen. In allen Zimmern sticht die weiße Farbe und das helle Eichenfurnier hervor, das diesen mehr Licht verleiht.

Dit appartement in Amsterdam is interessant vanwege de visuele continuïteit van de ruimtes. Zelfs de slaapkamer staat in verbinding met de andere vertrekken. De kleur wit komt in de hele woning terug, in combinatie met licht eikenfineer om het gevoel van licht te versterken.

Este apartamento situado en la ciudad de Ámsterdam llama la atención por la continuidad visual de sus espacios. Incluso un ambiente tan privado como el cuarto de baño también se halla abierto a las demás dependencias. En todas las habitaciones destaca el color blanco y los enchapados en roble claro para aumentar la luminosidad.

Questo appartamento sito nella città di Amsterdam sorprende per la continuità visiva dei suoi spazi. Perfino un contesto così intimo come il bagno è aperto alle altre stanze. In tutti gli ambienti spiccano il colore bianco e i laminati di rovere chiaro per aumentare la luminosità.

Este apartamento situado na cidade de Amesterdão é espectacular pela continuidade visual dos espaços que o conformam. Mesmo um ambiente tão íntimo e privado como o quarto-de-banho se encontra aberto às restantes divisões. O branco e os contraplacados em carvalho claro predominam em todos os aposentos para aumentar a luminosidade.

Denna våning i Amsterdam är intressant på grund av den visuella kontinuiteten mellan utrymmena. Till och med ett område så privat som badrummet är öppet mot de andra rummen. Färgen vit är genomgående dominant i fastigheten med blek ekfanér för att öka känslan av ljus.

1. Entrance
2. Kitchen
3. Living room
4. Terrace
5. Bedroom
6. Bathroom
7. Rest room

Plan

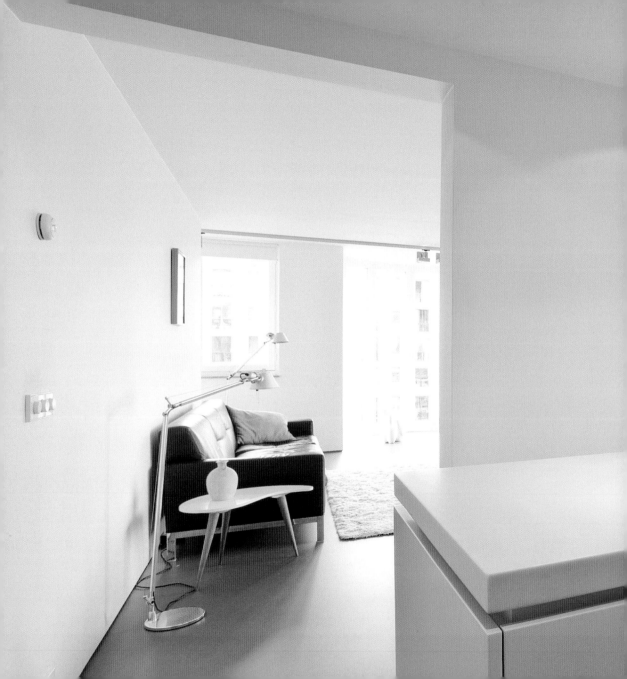

FONTANA HOUSE

N MAEDA ATELIER
© Shin Fhoto Work

Maeda's inspiration for the design of this house was the work of plastic artist Lucio Fontana, which consists of holes or slits in the canvases of his paintings. In the house, this system created large, integrated spaces and incorporated the garden with the interior, which has plenty of natural light due to the large number of windows.

L'œuvre du plasticien Lucio Fontana, qui perce ses toiles de fentes et de trous, a inspiré Maeda pour la conception de cette maison. Il a ainsi imaginé de vastes espaces intégrés et incorporé le jardin à l'intérieur, baigné de lumière naturelle grâce à de multiples ouvertures.

Für den Entwurf dieses Einfamilienhauses hat sich Maeda vom Werk des plastischen Künstlers Lucio Fontana inspirieren lassen, der die Leinwand seiner Bilder mit Löchern und Einschnitten versieht. Diese Methode spiegelt sich in dem weitgefassten, ganzheitlichen Innendesign wider, der Garten wurde in das Innere verlegt und erhält aufgrund der zahlreichen Glasöffnungen ausreichend natürliches Licht.

Maeda's inspiratie voor het ontwerp van dit huis was het werk van beeldend kunstenaar Lucio Fontana, dat bestaat schilderijen met gaten of spleten. In het huis leidde deze inspiratiebron tot grote, geïntegreerde ruimtes. De tuin is opgenomen in het interieur, dat dankzij de vele ramen overgoten wordt met daglicht.

Maeda diseñó esta casa unifamiliar inspirándose en la obra del artista plástico Lucio Fontana, consistente en agujeros o tajos sobre la tela de sus pinturas. En la casa, este sistema creó ambientes amplios e integrados e incorporó el jardín al interior, que recibe abundante luz natural debido a la gran cantidad de aberturas de cristal.

Maeda ha progettato questa casa unifamiliare ispirandosi alle opere dell'artista plastico Lucio Fontana, consistenti in buchi o tagli praticati sulle tele dei suoi quadri. Nella casa, grazie a questo sistema, da una parte, sono stati creati ambienti ampi e integrati, mentre dall'altra, il giardino è stato incorporato allo spazio interno, che riceve luce naturale in abbondanza per la gran quantità di porte e finestre di vetro.

Maeda concebeu esta casa unifamiliar inspirando-se na obra do artista plástico Lucio Fontana, cujos quadros pintados estão repletos de buracos e cortes na tela. Na casa, este sistema criou ambientes amplos e integrados: o jardim foi incorporado no interior, que recebe abundante luz natural devido à grande quantidade de aberturas de vidro.

Maedas inspiration till designen på detta hus var verk av plastartisten Lucio Fontana, som bestå av hål eller revor i duken på hans tavlor. I huset skapade detta system stora, integrerade utrymmer och inkorporerade trädgården med interiören som har massor av naturligt ljus tack vare det stora antalet fönster.

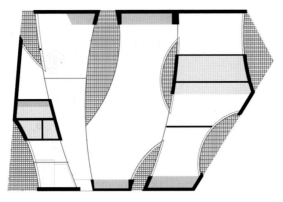

First floor

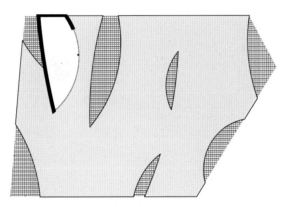

Second floor

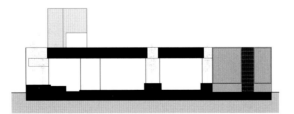

Section

LORDS TELEPHONE EXCHANGE

PASKIN KYRIAKIDES SANDS
© Paskin Kyriakides Sands

The conversion of the Lords Telephone Exchange offices to create thirty-six residential units, including five lofts, resulted in open, spacious apartments. Inside, the windows and recesses in the walls visually connect the different spaces.

Les bureaux du Lords Telephone Exchange ont été transformés en trente-six appartements spacieux, dont cinq lofts. Les ouvertures intérieures et les recoins dans les murs relient visuellement les différents espaces.

Nach dem Umbau der Lords Telephone Exchange-Büroräume in sechsunddreißig Wohneinheiten, unter ihnen fünf Lofts, entstanden geräumige, offen wirkende Appartements. Im Inneren verbinden die Löcher in Wänden und Fenstern die Räume optisch miteinander.

De verbouwing van de kantoorruimtes van de Lords Telephone Exchanges tot zesendertig woningen, waaronder vijf lofts, heeft geresulteerd in open, ruime appartementen. Binnen vormen de ramen en nissen in de muren een visuele verbinding tussen de vertrekken.

La conversión de las oficinas de Lords Telephone Exchange en treinta y seis unidades residenciales, incluidos cinco lofts, dio como resultado unos apartamentos abiertos y de espacios voluminosos. En el interior, los huecos en las paredes y las ventanas conectan visualmente un ambiente con otro.

La conversione degli uffici del Lords Telephone Exchange in trentasei unità residenziali, inclusi cinque loft, ha dato come risultato alcuni appartamenti aperti e spazi voluminosi. All'interno, le aperture nelle pareti e le finestre creano un legame visivo tra un ambiente e l'altro.

A transformação dos escritórios da Lords Telephone Exchange em trinta e seis unidades residenciais, incluindo cinco lofts, teve como resultado uns apartamentos abertos e de grandes espaços. No interior, as aberturas nas paredes e nas janelas estabelecem uma ligação entre os vários ambientes.

Ombyggnaden av Lords telefonväxelkontor för att skapa 36 boendeenheter, inklusive fem loft, resulterade i öppna, rymliga lägenheter. På insidan förbinder fönstren och alkoverna visuellt de olika utrymmena.

Elevation

General plans

SARRIÀ SAMSÓ DUPLEX

EDUARD SAMSÓ
© Jordi Miralles

This loft is located in a five-storey apartment building. At the center of the design is a U-shaped living room in which the floor, wall and ceiling are covered in wood. This area is visually separated from the kitchen by a grey sofa with yellow and orange Egg chairs.

Ce loft se trouve dans un bâtiment de quatre étages. Le salon en U occupe le centre de ce volume dont les sols, les murs et le plafond sont habillés de bois. L'espace de vie est séparé de la cuisine par le canapé gris et les chaises ovoïdes jaunes et orange.

Dieses Loft befindet sich in einem fünfstöckigen Wohngebäude. Im Mittelpunkt dieses Entwurfs steht der U-förmige Wohnzimmerbereich mit seiner Holzverkleidung am Boden, auf der Wand und den Decken. Optisch wurde er von der Küche durch ein graues Sofa und Egg-Stühlen in Gelb und Orange abgetrennt.

Deze loft bevindt zich in een appartementencomplex van vijf verdiepingen. Een U-vormige woonkamer, waarin vloer, wand en plafond met hout zijn afgewerkt, vormt de kern van het ontwerp. Deze ruimte wordt visueel van de keuken gescheiden door een grijze bank en gele en oranje Egg Chairs.

Este loft se encuentra en un edificio de apartamentos de cinco plantas. El centro de este diseño es la zona del salón en forma de U, con el suelo, la pared y el techo revestidos de madera. Está separado visualmente de la zona de la cocina por un sofá gris y unas sillas Egg amarillas y naranjas.

Questo loft si trova in un palazzo di appartamenti di cinque piani. L'elemento centrale del progetto è la zona del soggiorno a forma di U, con il pavimento, la parete e il soffitto rivestiti di legno. È visivamente separato dalla zona della cucina per mezzo di un sofà grigio e di sedie Egg gialle e arancione.

Este loft encontra-se num edifício de apartamentos de cinco andares. O núcleo central do projecto é a zona da sala em forma de U, com o chão, a parede e o tecto revestidos a madeira. Este espaço está visualmente separado da zona da cozinha por um sofá cinzento com umas cadeiras Egg amarelas e cor-de-laranja.

Detta loft ligger i ett femvåningshus med lägenheter. I mitten av designen finns ett u-format vardagsrum i vilket golv, väggar och tak är täckt med trä. Detta utrymme är visuellt separerat från köket av en grå soffa med gula och orange Ägget-fåtöljer.

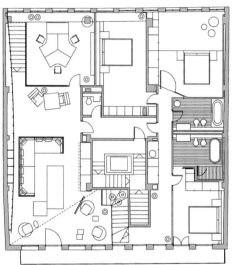

Ground floor

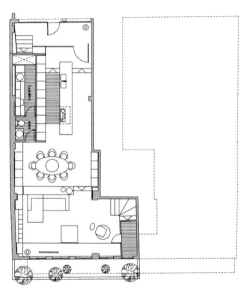

First floor

VALLIRANA

JOAN ORTEGA GARCÍA
© José Luis Hausmann

This newly-built house has a clearly minimalist style, both in the architecture and in the decoration. With straight lines and a predominance of white and neutral tones, the decoration brings personality to each of the rooms.

De construction récente, cette maison embrasse le minimalisme, autant dans son architecture que pour sa décoration. Les lignes sont droites, le blanc et les tons neutres dominent et font ressortir la personnalité de chaque pièce.

Architektur und Dekoration dieses neu erbauten Einfamilienhauses liegen ganz auf der Linie des minimalistischen Trends. Die Dekoration verleiht mit ihren klaren Linien, und überwiegend weißen und neutralen Tönen, den Räumen eine sehr persönliche Note.

Dit pasgebouwde huis heeft duidelijk een minimalistische stijl, zowel qua architectuur als qua inrichting. Met rechte lijnen en veel witte en neutrale tinten geeft de inrichting elk vertrek persoonlijkheid.

Esta vivienda, unifamiliar y de nueva construcción, responde de forma contundente, tanto en su arquitectura como en su decoración, a la tendencia minimalista. Con líneas rectas y predominio del color blanco y las tonalidades neutras, la decoración otorga personalidad a cada uno de los ambientes.

Questa casa, unifamiliare e di nuova costruzione, è una decisa risposta alla tendenza minimalista, tanto nella sua architettura quanto nella decorazione. Con linee rette e predominio del colore bianco e dei toni neutri, la decorazione dà personalità a tutti i singoli ambienti.

Quer do ponto de vista da arquitectura quer do da decoração, esta vivenda unifamiliar construída de raiz tem uma tendência claramente minimalista. Com linhas rectas e predominância de branco e de tons pastel, a decoração confere personalidade a cada um dos ambientes.

Detta nybyggda hus har en klart minimalistisk stil både i arkitekturen och i inredningen. Med raka linjer och dominans av vita och naturliga toner skänker inredningen personlighet till vart och ett av rummen.

AZUL TIERRA HOUSE

C & C ESTUDIO
© José Luis Hausmann

This recently renovated house is located only 15 meters from the sea. The new style is clearly modern and Mediterranean, with a predominance of straight lines and white. The decorative accessories, also with connections to the sea, create a perfect Mediterranean ambiance in the house.

Cette maison récemment rénovée n'est qu'à une quinzaine de mètres du rivage. Elle arbore un style résolument moderne et méditerranéen, souligné par les droites épurées et le blanc. La déco d'inspiration marine souligne l'ambiance de la maison.

Dieses vor kurzem umgestaltete Haus liegt nur fünfzehn Meter vom Meer entfernt. Sein neuer Stil ist mediterran und modern, wobei seine geraden Linien und seine weiße Farbe besonders dominant sind. Mit der Wahl des Dekorzubehörs wurde auch im Inneren des Hauses mediterrane Stimmung geschaffen.

Dit recent verbouwde huis bevindt zich slechts 15 meter van de zee. De nieuwe stijl is duidelijk modern en mediterraan, met veel rechte lijnen en wit. De accessoires, die eveneens een link met de zee vormen, creëren een perfecte mediterrane sfeer in het huis.

Esta vivienda, recientemente remodelada, se encuentra a tan sólo unos quince metros del mar. El nuevo estilo es claramente mediterráneo y moderno, predominando las líneas rectas y el color blanco. Los complementos de decoración, también relacionados con el mar, crean un perfecto clima mediterráneo en el hogar.

Questa casa, ristrutturata di recente, sorge appena a una quindicina di metri dal mare. Il nuovo stile è chiaramente mediterraneo e moderno, con egemonia delle linee rette e del colore bianco. Gli accessori decorativi, anch'essi legati al mare, creano un perfetto clima mediterraneo nella casa.

Esta vivienda, recentemente remodelada, encontra-se a apenas quinze metros do mar. Tem um estilo claramente mediterrânico e moderno, em que predominam as linhas rectas e o branco. Os complementos da decoração, também relacionados com o mar, criam uma perfeita atmosfera mediterrânica.

Detta nyligen renoverade hus ligger endast 15 meter från havet. Den nya stilen är klart modern och medelhavsinspirerad med en dominans av raka linjer och vitt. De dekorativa accessoarerna, även med koppling till havet, skapar en perfekt medelhavsstämning i huset.

336

LOFT BY **KARIM RASHID**

Designed as just one space, this New York loft has simply the walls strictly necessary to define the only two rooms – the bedroom and the bathroom. The rest of the apartment is an open space where bright colors and the constant search for new combinations predominate.

Conçu comme un espace unique, ce loft new-yorkais a juste assez de murs pour définir les deux pièces, la chambre et la salle de bains. Le reste de l'appartement est un espace ouvert où dominent les couleurs vives et la recherche d'associations osées.

Da es als Einzelraum gestaltet ist, wurden in diesem *Loft* in New York nur jene Wände gezogen, die für die Abtrennung der zwei einzigen vorhandenen Zimmer absolut unabkömmlich waren: das Schlafzimmer und das Bad. Der restliche Raum wurde als offener, zusammengehöriger Bereich konzipiert, in dem die auffallenden Farben und die konstante Suche nach neuen Kombinationen hervorstechen.

Deze loft in New York is als één ruimte ontworpen en bevat alleen de muren die strikt noodzakelijk zijn om de enige twee kamers af te scheiden: de slaapkamer en de badkamer. De rest is één open ruimte waarin felle kleuren en interessante combinaties overheersen.

Proyectado como un espacio único, este *loft* en Nueva York carece de paredes más allá de las estrictamente necesarias para definir las dos únicas habitaciones existentes: el dormitorio y el baño. El resto se ha concebido como un espacio abierto donde destacan los colores llamativos y la búsqueda constante de nuevas combinaciones.

Progettato come uno spazio unico, questo *loft* di New York ha solo le pareti strettamente necessarie per definire le uniche due stanze esistenti: la camera da letto e il bagno. Il resto è stato concepito come uno spazio aperto in cui spiccano i colori vivi e la ricerca costante di nuove combinazioni.

Projectado como um espaço único, este *loft* de Nova Iorque não tem paredes além das estritamente necessárias para definir os dois únicos quartos existentes: o quarto de dormir e o quarto-de-banho. O resto foi concebido como um espaço aberto em que se destacam as cores apelativas e a constante procura de novas combinações.

Designat som endast ett utrymme har detta loft i New York helt enkelt enbart de nödvändigaste väggarna för att definiera de två rummen – sovrummet och badrummet. Resten av lägenheten är ett öppet utrymme där ljusa färger och det ständiga sökandet efter nya kombinationer dominerar.

VALLVIDRERA HOUSE

ESTUDIO INTERIORISMO ADELA CABRÉ
© Jordi Miralles

This design was to turn a building constructed at the beginning of the 20th century into a new home for a family of three. It was decided to restore parts of the wall in the staircase area, which had been under a layer of plaster. The decoration is somber, with black and white chosen as the base colors in most of the rooms.

L'objectif était de transformer un bâtiment du début du xxe siècle en une maison confortable pour une famille de trois personnes. Le pan de mur en briques de la cage d'escalier, autrefois caché par une couche de plâtre, a été remis à nu et restauré. La décoration est sombre, et l'association de blanc et noir domine dans la plupart des pièces.

In diesem Fall wurde ein am Anfang des 20. Jahrhunderts erbautes Gebäude in das Zuhause einer dreiköpfigen Familie umgestaltet. Teile der sich im Stiegenbereich befindlichen Wand wurden mit einer Gipsschicht restauriert. Die Dekoration ist karg gehalten, als Grundfarben wählte man für die Mehrzahl der Räume Weiß und Schwarz.

Dit ontwerp moest van een pand uit begin 20e eeuw een moderne gezinswoning maken. Er is gekozen om delen van de muur bij de trap, die waren bedekt met een pleisterlaag, weer zichtbaar te maken. De inrichting is sober, met zwart en wit als basiskleuren.

En este diseño, un edificio construido a comienzos del siglo xx se convirtió en el nuevo hogar de una familia de tres miembros. Se decidió restaurar partes de la pared en la zona de escaleras bajo una capa de yeso. La decoración es austera y se han elegido el blanco y el negro como colores base para la mayoría de los ambientes.

In questo progetto, un edificio costruito agli inizi del xx secolo è stato trasformato nella nuova casa di una famiglia di tre persone. Si è deciso di restaurare alcune parti della parete nella zona delle scale sotto uno strato di gesso. La decorazione è austera e il bianco e il nero sono stati scelti come colori di base per la maggior parte degli ambienti.

Aqui, transformou-se um edificio construído no princípio do século XX num novo lar para uma família de três membros. Optou-se por restaurar partes da parede na zona de escadas sob uma camada de estuque. A decoração é austera e o branco e o preto foram as cores escolhidas como tónica para a maioria dos ambientes.

Denna design syftade till att förvandla en byggnad uppförd i början av 1900-talet till ett nytt hem åt en familj på tre. Det beslutades att renovera delar av väggen i trapphuset, som fanns under ett lager puts. Inredningen är sober med svart och vitt som valda basfärger i de flesta rum.

356

Second floor

Ground floor

First floor

TERRASSA PROJECT

EULALIA SARDÀ
© José Luis Hausmann

This house stands out for its modern aspect and the young spirit of the design. The owner wanted a space in which to live but also one in which to host dinners and parties with friends. Consequently a swimming pool and terrace were essential. The decorative elements have been carefully chosen by the owner, based on personal taste and comfort.

C'est le côté moderne et la jeunesse du design qui ressortent dans cette maison. Les propriétaires voulaient un espace de vie, mais aussi un lieu où recevoir leurs amis à dîner et où faire la fête. Il était donc essentiel de prévoir une piscine et une terrasse. Tous les objets ont été personnellement choisis par le propriétaire et reflètent donc ses goûts et son idée du confort.

An diesem Haus stechen seine Modernität und sein jugendlicher Stil hervor. Den Wünschen der Besitzerin entsprechend sollte dieser Wohnraum auch die Möglichkeit bieten, Abendessen und Feste mit Freunden zu veranstalten. Daher konnten ein Schwimmbad und eine Terrasse nicht fehlen. Die Dekorationselemente hat die Besitzerin selbst gewählt, sie spiegeln deren Geschmack und Wunsch nach Bequemlichkeit wider.

Dit huis valt op door zijn moderne uitstraling. De eigenaar wilde een ruimte om in te wonen, maar ook om etentjes en feestjes te geven. Daarom waren een zwembad en een terras essentieel. De decoratieve elementen zijn zorgvuldig door de eigenaar gekozen, gebaseerd op persoonlijke smaak en comfort.

Esta casa destaca por su modernidad y espíritu juvenil. La propietaria deseaba un espacio que sirviera tanto para habitar como para celebrar cenas y fiestas con amigos. Por ello, no podía faltar una piscina y una terraza. Los elementos de la decoración han sido cuidadosamente elegidos por la propietaria basándose en su gusto y comodidad.

Questa casa spicca per la sua modernità e il suo spirito giovane. La proprietaria voleva uno spazio che servisse sia come abitazione sia come luogo per organizzare cene e feste con amici. Per questa ragione, non potevano mancare una piscina e una terrazza. Gli elementi che fanno parte della decorazione sono stati scelti con estrema cura dalla proprietaria secondo il suo gusto e in base a un criterio di comodità.

Esta casa destaca-se pela nota de modernidade e pelo seu espírito jovial. A proprietária pretendia um espaço que servisse simultaneamente para ser habitado e para organizar jantares e festas com amigos. Assim sendo, não podia faltar uma piscina e uma esplanada. Os elementos da decoração foram cuidadosamente escolhidos pela proprietária de acordo com o gosto e a comodidade da mesma.

Detta hus sticker ut på grund av dess moderna aspekt och den unga andan i designen. Ägaren ville ha ett utrymme att leva i, men också ett där det går att hålla middagar och fester med vänner. Följaktligen var en swimmingpool och en terrass nödvändiga. De dekorativa inslagen har valts omsorgsfullt av ägaren, baserat på personlig smak och komfort.

First plan

Second plan

KELSO HOUSE

ARCHITECTS EAT
© Shania Shegedyn

In order to find a harmonious balance between the need for natural light and the need for privacy, strips of glass were installed in the roof and glass doors in the façade overlooking the garden. Chairs in different shapes, colors, materials and textures were carefully chosen to decorate the most commonly used areas.

Afin de trouver un équilibre harmonieux entre la lumière naturelle et le besoin d'intimité, des bandes vitrées ont été aménagées dans la toiture et sur les portes de la façade qui donne sur le jardin. Les pièces de vie sont meublées de chaises de formes, de couleurs, de matériaux et de textures différents.

Um einen harmonischen Kompromiss zwischen dem notwendigen natürlichen Lichteinfall und der erwünschten Intimsphäre zu erreichen, wurden auf dem Dach Glasstreifen und verglaste Türen in der gartenseitigen Fassade eingebaut. Verschiedenartig geformte Stühle, vielseitige Materialien und Texturen wurden für die Dekoration der am häufigsten frequentierten Bereiche mit großer Sorgfalt ausgesucht.

Om een evenwicht te vinden tussen de behoefte aan daglicht en privacy, zijn er stroken glas in het dak geplaatst en glazen deuren in de gevel aan de tuinzijde. Stoelen in verschillende vormen, kleuren, materialen en texturen zijn met zorg gekozen als inrichting voor de meest gebruikte vertrekken.

Para encontrar una solución armoniosa entre la necesidad de luz natural y la privacidad deseada, se idearon unas franjas de cristal en el tejado y huecos de puerta acristalados en la fachada lindante al jardín. Sillas de diferentes formas, colores, materiales y texturas se seleccionaron cuidadosamente para decorar las áreas de mayor tránsito.

Per trovare una soluzione armonica tra il bisogno di luce naturale e la desiderata privacy, sono stati concepiti dei parapetti di vetro sul tetto e nei vani delle porte a vetri sulla facciata confinante con il giardino. Sedie di varie forme, colori, materiali e texture sono state scelte con molta cura per decorare le zone di maggior transito.

Para encontrar uma solução harmoniosa entre a necessidade de luz natural e a privacidade desejada, foram criadas umas faixas de vidro no telhado e portas envidraçadas na fachada que dá para o jardim. Foram cuidadosamente escolhidas cadeiras de várias formas, cores, materiais e texturas para decorar as áreas de maior concentração de pessoas.

För att hitta en harmonisk balans mellan behovet av naturligt ljus och behovet av avskildhet installerades remsor av glas i yttertaket och glasdörrar i fasaden som vetter mot trädgården. Stolar i olika former, färger, material och texturer valdes noggrant för att dekorera de mest använda områdena.

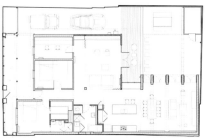

Plan

JOHN BARMAN RESIDENCE

This apartment was erected on an original modernist building, built in 1959, which houses offices. During the renovation process the interior architecture was streamlined to create a modern, personal atmosphere. The predominating color palette is characterized by strong contrasts between red and white.

Cet appartement a été bâti dans un édifice construit en 1959 dans un style résolument moderne et qui abrite des bureaux. Lors des travaux de rénovation, l'architecture intérieure a été redéfinie et des cloisons supprimées pour créer une atmosphère contemporaine personnalisée. La palette est dominée par le rouge et le blanc qui forment de violents contrastes.

Das Appartement wurde über einer aus dem Jahre 1959 stammenden Struktur erbaut, die früher Büroräume beherbergte. Die Umgestaltung des Innenraums verfolgte das Ziel, eine moderne und persönliche Atmosphäre zu schaffen. Die vorwiegenden farblichen Tonalitäten zeigen starke Kontraste zwischen Rot und Weiß.

Dit appartement is gebouwd op een origineel modernistisch gebouw uit 1959, waarin kantoren gevestigd zijn. Tijdens de verbouwing werd het interieur gestroomlijnd om een moderne, persoonlijke sfeer te creëren. Het kleurenpalet wordt gekenmerkt door krachtige contrasten tussen rood en wit.

El apartamento se erige sobre una estructura modernista original de 1959 que albergaba oficinas. En el proceso de remodelación se racionalizó la arquitectura interior para crear un ambiente moderno y personal. La paleta de colores predominante se caracteriza por los fuertes contrastes entre el rojo y el blanco.

L'appartamento sorge su una struttura modernista originale del 1959 che ospitava uffici. Nel processo di ristrutturazione è stata razionalizzata l'architettura degli interni per creare un ambiente moderno e personale. La gamma cromatica predominante è caratterizzata da forti contrasti tra il rosso e il bianco.

O apartamento fica situado sobre uma estrutura modernista original de 1959 que albergava escritórios. No processo de remodelação, racionalizou-se a arquitectura interior para criar um ambiente moderno e pessoal. A paleta de cores predominante é fortemente marcada pelo contraste entre o vermelho e o branco.

Denna våning uppfördes på en originell modernistisk byggnad, byggd 1959, som hyser kontor. Genom renoveringsprocessen strömlinjeformades interiörens arkitektur för att skapa en modern personlig atmosfär. Den dominerande färgpaletten karaktäriseras av starka kontraster mellan rött och vitt.

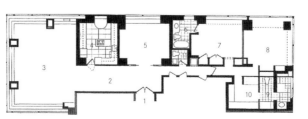

Plan

1. Entrance
2. Corridor
3. Living room
4. Kitchen
5. Dining room
6. Bathroom
7. Library
8. Bedroom
9. Bathroom
10. Dressing room
11. Bathroom

MAISON

VAN DER MERWE MISZEWSKI ARCHITECTS
© Van der Merwe Miszewski Architects

This property was built on a lot measuring 10 hectares, in the heart of the Franschhoek Valley. The project included re-using the farm, surrounded by magnificent old oak trees. The large living room accommodates white sofas and chairs, which contrast with the colorful surrounding countryside.

Le bâtiment se situe sur un terrain de 10 hectares au cœur de la Franschhoek Valley. Il s'agissait de recréer un lieu de vie dans cette ferme entourée de magnifiques vieux chênes. Le large salon est meublé de canapés et de chaises blancs, ce qui contraste avec les teintes vives de la campagne environnante.

Das Projekt erhebt sich auf einem zehn Hektar großen Grundstück, im Herzen des Franschhoektals. Der Designentwurf sollte die Wiedernutzung des von alten, prächtigen Eichen umgebenen Landguts einschließen. Das durch seine Weite hervorstechende Wohnzimmer bot genügend Platz, um weiße Sofas und Armsessel aufzustellen, die mit den Farben der umgebenden Landschaft einen herrlichen Kontrast bilden.

Dit huis is gebouwd op een kavel van 10 hectare in het hart van de Franschhoekvallei. Het project omvatte tevens het hergebruik van de boerderij, die is omringd door schitterende oude bomen. In de grote woonkamer staan witte banken en stoelen, die contrasteren met het kleurrijke omringende platteland.

El proyecto se levanta en un terreno de 10 hectáreas de extensión, en el corazón del valle Franschhoek. El alcance de la propuesta incluyó la reutilización de la granja, rodeada de antiguos y magníficos robles. La gran amplitud del salón permitió colocar un juego de sofás y sillones de color blanco para contrastar con el colorido que otorga el paisaje.

Il progetto sorge su un terreno di 10 ettari d'estensione, nel cuore stesso della valle Franschhoek. La proposta ha previsto il riutilizzo della fattoria, circondata da antiche e splendide querce. La grande ampiezza del soggiorno ha permesso di porre un insieme di sofà e poltrone di colore bianco per creare un forte contrasto con le tonalità cromatiche date dal paesaggio.

O projecto foi construído num terreno de 10 hectares, no coração do vale de Franschhoek. O alcance da proposta incluiu a reutilização da quinta, rodeada de carvalhos antigos e magníficos. A extensão da sala permitiu colocar um jogo de sofás e cadeirões brancos, para contrastar com o colorido da paisagem.

Denna egendom byggdes på en tomt på 10 hektar i hjärtat av Franschhoek-dalen. Projektet innefattade att återanvända gården, omgiven av magnifika gamla ekar. Det stora vardagsrummet rymmer vita soffor och stolar som kontrasterar mot den färgstarka omgivande landsbygden.

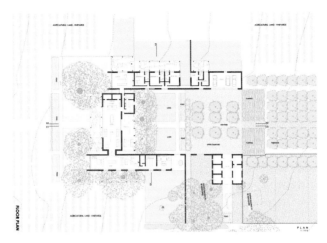

Floor plan

Sections

Elevations

KLANG APARTMENT

This project reflects the designers' desire to counteract hectic city life. Light plays a determining role: it creates spaces which are almost theatrical and provides a certain drama in the property, which is dominated by a range of warm tones and natural textures. The furnishings are also inspired by nature.

Il est aisé de lire dans cet intérieur la volonté de s'opposer au rythme effréné de la vie urbaine. La lumière joue un rôle déterminant : elle crée des espaces presque scéniques qui impriment au lieu une certaine théâtralité. Les tons chauds et les fibres naturelles dominent. Le mobilier s'inspire lui aussi de la nature.

Das Projekt spiegelt den Wunsch der Planer, einen Kontrast zur schnelllebigen Stadt zu schaffen, wieder. Dem Licht kommt eine besondere Bedeutung zu: mit seiner Hilfe werden nahezu theatralisch wirkende Räume geschaffen, in denen warme Farben und natürliche Texturen dominieren. Auch das Mobiliar zieht seine Inspiration aus der Natur.

Doel van de ontwerpers was een rustige thuishaven te creëren in de drukke stad. Het licht speelt een grote rol: het creëert ruimtes die bijna theatraal zijn en geeft de woning iets speciaals. Verder wordt de sfeer bepaald door warme tinten en natuurlijke texturen. Ook het meubilair is geïnspireerd door de natuur.

El proyecto refleja el deseo de los diseñadores de contrarrestar la agitada vida de la ciudad. La luz juega un papel determinante: crea espacios casi teatrales y proporciona cierto dramatismo al ambiente, dominado por una gama de tonos cálidos y texturas naturales. El mobiliario también está inspirado en la naturaleza.

Questo progetto rispecchia il desiderio dei progettisti di porre una barriera alla frenetica vita della città. La luce vi gioca un ruolo determinante: crea spazi quasi teatrali e fornisce una certa drammaticità all'ambiente, dominato da una gamma di tonalità calde e texture naturali. Anche l'arredamento è ispirato alla natura.

O projecto reflecte a vontade dos designers de compensar a agitada vida da cidade. A luz desempenha um papel determinante: cria espaços quase teatrais e proporciona um certo dramatismo ao ambiente, dominado por uma gama de tons quentes e texturas naturais. A natureza também inspirou a escolha do mobiliário.

Detta projekt reflekterar designernas önskan att motverka det hektiska stadslivet. Ljus spelar en avgörande roll: det skapar utrymmen som är närmast teatraliska och bidrar med ett visst drama i fastigheten som domineras av en skala av varma toner och naturliga texturer. Möblerna är också inspirerade av naturen.

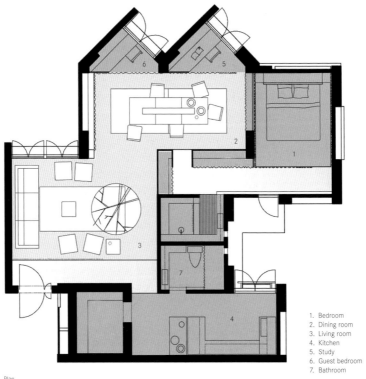

Plan

1. Bedroom
2. Dining room
3. Living room
4. Kitchen
5. Study
6. Guest bedroom
7. Bathroom

NÚRIA AMAT HOUSE

JORDI GARCÉS ARQUITECTES
© Jordi Miralles

The main objective was that the house should form part of the rough cliff on which it is located, but at the same time should be comfortable for those living there. The interior design was carried out by the owner, who carefully selected the furnishings and accessories, with a tendency towards black and white.

Il fallait que cette villa semble faire partie de la falaise sur laquelle elle est construite tout en offrant un intérieur confortable à ses occupants. C'est le propriétaire qui s'est chargé d'imaginer la décoration intérieure et qui a choisi avec soin tous les meubles et objets. On remarque une préférence pour le noir et blanc.

Das Hauptziel bestand darin, die atemberaubenden umgebenden Klippen in das Design des Wohnraums einzubeziehen, diesen jedoch für seine Bewohner trotzdem komfortabel zu gestalten. Der Innenraum wurde von der Besitzerin selbst designed: Die Einrichtung und Zubehör wurden von ihr sorgsam ausgewählt, wobei sie zu den Farben Schwarz und Weiß tendierte.

Het huis moest als het ware opgaan in de ruwe klippen waarop het staat, maar moest wel comfortabel zijn voor zijn bewoners. Het interieurontwerp is uitgevoerd door de eigenaar, die de meubels en accessoires met zorg heeft gekozen, met een voorkeur voor zwart en wit.

El objetivo principal era que la vivienda compartiera la bravura del acantilado donde se encuentra emplazada, pero que a la vez resultara confortable para sus habitantes. El interiorismo lo llevó a cabo la misma propietaria: seleccionó cuidadosamente el mobiliario y los complementos, inclinándose por los colores blanco y negro.

Il principale scopo del progetto di è consistito nel dare la possibilità all'abitazione di condividere il carattere selvaggio della scogliera su cui sorge, ma, nel contempo, di essere confortevole per chi la abita. Il design degli interni è stato realizzato dalla proprietaria stessa, la quale ha scelto con cura l'arredamento e gli accessori, tendendo verso il bianco e il nero.

O objectivo principal era que a casa partilhasse a bravura do alcantilado em que se encontra situada, mas sem deixar de ser confortável para os seus habitantes. O interiorismo ficou a cargo da proprietária, que escolheu cuidadosamente o mobiliário e os complementos, privilegiando o branco e o preto.

Huvudmålet var att huset skulle utgöra en del av den ojämna klippan på vilken det är beläget, samtidigt som det skulle vara bekvämt för de som bor där. Designen på interiören genomfördes av ägaren som omsorgsfullt valde ut möblerna och accessoarerna med en tendens åt svart och vitt.

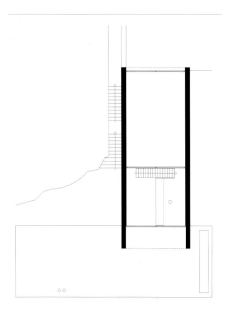

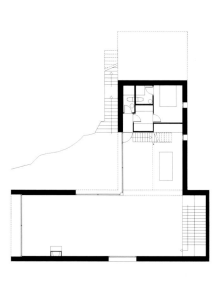

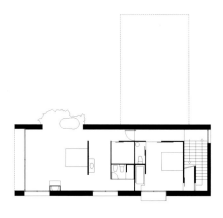

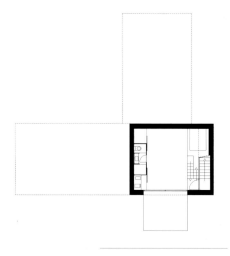

Floor plans

THE BRIDGE HOUSE

VAN DER MERWE MISZEWSKI ARCHITECTS
© Van der Merwe Miszewski Architects

With three adjacent parts forming one entity, this house is located on a steep slope. The property is situated on a dry river-bed, surrounded by exotic indigenous trees, and the entrance is reached through a door. The furnishings throughout the house are the Dutch brand Linteloo, which owns the house.

Cette maison se compose de trois parties mitoyennes qui forment un tout. Elle est située sur un terrain très pentu dans le lit d'une rivière asséchée où poussent des arbres exotiques indigènes. Il faut franchir une porte pour atteindre l'entrée. Tout le mobilier est de la marque hollandaise Linteloo, qui en est la propriétaire.

Bei diesem Haus formen drei aneinander anschließende Teile eine Einheit, es steht auf einer Steigung. Unter ihm verlauft ein eingetrocknetes Flussbett und ringsum wachsen exotische Bäume. Die Einrichtung im ganzen Haus stammt von Linteloo, einer holländischen Firma, in deren Eigentum der Besitz steht.

Dit huis, waarin drie aangrenzende delen één geheel vormen, staat op een steile helling, bij een droge rivierbedding. Het is omringd door inheemse bomen en de entree wordt via een deur bereikt. Alle meubels in het huis zijn van het Nederlandse merk Linteloo, dat eigenaar van het pand is.

Con tres partes adyacentes que forman una entidad única, esta casa está situada sobre una pendiente ascendente. La vivienda se sitúa sobre el cauce de un río seco, rodeado de árboles autóctonos y exóticos, y la entrada comunica con un puente. El mobiliario de toda la vivienda es de la marca holandesa Linteloo, dueña de esta propiedad.

Con tre parti adiacenti che formano un unico insieme, questa casa si trova su una pendenza e occupa un'area sul letto di un fiume asciutto, circondato da alberi autoctoni ed esotici, e l'ingresso comunica con un ponte. L'arredamento di tutta la casa è della marca olandese Linteloo, padrona di questa proprietà.

Esta casa com três partes adjacentes que formam uma entidade única fica situada numa encosta ascendente. A casa, rodeada de árvores autóctones e exóticas, encontra-se o leito de um rio seco, pelo que a entrada dá para uma ponte. O mobiliário é da marca holandesa Linteloo, pertencente à dona desta propriedade.

Med tre intilliggande delar som bildar en enhet är detta hus beläget på en brant sluttning. Fastigheten ligger på en torr flodbädd omgiven av exotiska inhemska träd och entrén nås genom en dörr. Möblerna i huset är av det holländska märket Linteloo, som äger huset.

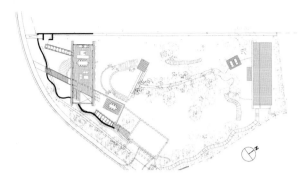

Upper floor

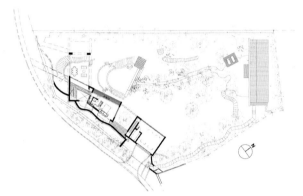

Middle floor

Site long section North-South

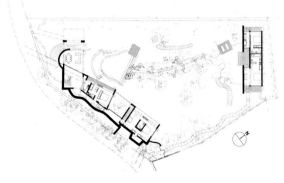

Lower floor

Developed external street facade

BLACK APARTMENT

THE APARTMENT CREATIVE AGENCY
© Michael Weber

The owner's wish to feel as if she was "in a bar in Shanghai as night falls" lead to the floor, walls and ceiling of this apartment being completely black. The owner saw this choice of color as an excellent opportunity to exhibit her eclectic collection of furniture, art, books, and shoes signed by their designers.

La propriétaire voulait pouvoir s'imaginer être dans un bar de Shanghai à la tombée de la nuit. Les sols, les murs et les plafonds sont entièrement noirs. Ce choix offre un écrin idéal pour mettre en valeur une collection éclectique de meubles, d'objets d'art, de livres et de chaussures signés par des créateurs.

Der Wunsch der Besitzerin, sich "bei Einfall der Nacht wie in einer Bar in Shanghai" zu fühlen, wurde in diesem Appartement mit völlig schwarzen Wänden, Decken und Böden, Wirklichkeit. Die Besitzerin nahm die hervorragende Gelegenheit wahr, die ihr die Wahl der Farbe bot, um ihre eklektische Kollektion an von ihren Erschaffern signierten Möbeln, Kunstobjekten, Büchern und Schuhen, auszustellen.

De wens het gevoel te hebben om 'bij het vallen van de avond in een bar in Shanghai te zitten' heeft ertoe geleid dat de vloer, wanden en het plafond van dit appartement zwart zijn. Hierdoor kan de eigenares haar verzameling meubels, kunst, boeken en door hun ontwerpers gesigneerde schoenen prachtig tentoonstellen.

El deseo de la propietaria de sentirse como «en un bar de Shanghai al caer la noche» tomó la forma de un apartamento de paredes, techos y suelo completamente negros. La dueña vio en la elección del color una excelente oportunidad para exhibir su ecléctica colección de muebles, arte, libros y zapatos firmados por diseñadores.

Il desiderio della proprietaria di sentirsi come «in un bar di Shanghai quando cala la notte» si è concretizzato in un appartamento con pareti, soffitti e pavimento completamente neri. La proprietaria ha considerato la scelta di questo colore come un'eccellente opportunità per mostrare la sua eclettica collezione di mobili, opere d'arte, libri e scarpe firmate da stilisti.

A vontade da proprietária de se sentir «num bar de Xangai ao cair da noite» deu origem a um apartamento com paredes, tectos e chão completamente pretos. A dona viu na selecção da cor uma excelente oportunidade para exibir a sua colecção de móveis, arte, livros e sapatos assinados por designers.

Ägarens önskan att känna det som om hon vore "på en bar i Shanghai när natten faller på" ledde till att golvet, väggarna oh taket i denna våning blev helt svarta. Ägaren detta färgval som ett utmärkt tillfälle att visa upp sin vidsynta samling av möbler, konst, böcker och skor signerade av sina designers.

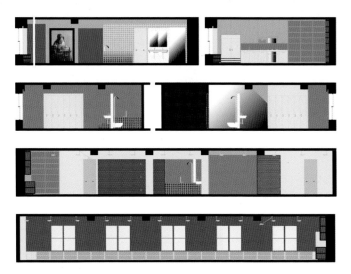

Sections

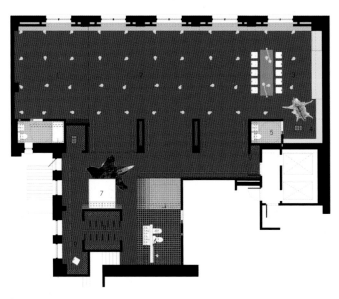

1. Library
2. Living room
3. Dining room
4. Kitchen
5. Bathroom
6. Bathroom
7. Bedroom
8. Closet
9. Rest room

Plan

STEVE HOUSE

MARCO SAVORELLI
© Matteo Piazza

This house was completely renovated to bring all its different functions together in just one space. The dividing walls were demolished and the doors were replaced with movable panels which, when closed, look as if they are the walls. The specially designed furnishings were made in lacquered rosewood.

Cette maison a été entièrement rénovée pour concentrer toutes ses différentes fonctions en un seul espace. Les cloisons ont été supprimées et les portes remplacées par des panneaux mobiles qui, quand ils sont fermés, donnent l'impression de former un mur. Les meubles créés sur commande sont en bois de rose laqué.

Dieser Wohnraum wurde komplett neu renoviert, um einen einzigen Allzweckraum zu schaffen. Die Zwischenwände wurden niedergerissen und durch Schiebepaneele ersetzt, die in geschlossenem Zustand als in die Wand integriert erscheinen. Das eigens entworfene Mobiliar wurde in lackiertem Rosenholz ausgeführt.

Dit huis is volledig verbouwd om alle functies bijeen te brengen in slechts één ruimte. De scheidingswanden werden gesloopt en de deuren vervangen door verplaatsbare panelen die er, als ze gesloten zijn, uitzien als wanden. De speciaal ontworpen meubels zijn van gelakt rozenhout.

Este espacio sufrió una renovación completa para unificar todas sus funciones en un único ambiente. Se derribaron las paredes divisorias y las puertas se reemplazaron por paneles móviles que, una vez cerrados, quedan integrados en las paredes. El mobiliario, diseñado especialmente, fue realizado en madera lacada de palo de rosa.

Questo spazio è stato completamente rinnovato per unificare tutte le sue funzioni in un solo ambiente. Sono state abbattute le pareti divisorie, mentre le porte sono state sostituite da pannelli scorrevoli che, una volta chiusi, restano all'interno dei muri. L'arredamento, espressamente ideato per questa casa, è stato realizzato in legno laccato di palo di rosa.

Este espaço sofreu uma renovação completa para concentrar todas as suas funções num único ambiente. Derrubaram-se paredes provisórias e as portas foram substituídas por painéis móveis que, uma vez fechados, se integram nas paredes. O mobiliário especialmente desenhado foi realizado em madeira lacada de pau-rosa.

Detta hus renoverades fullständigt för att sammanför alla dess olika funktioner i endast ett utrymme. De avdelande väggarna revs och dörrarna ersattes av flyttbara paneler som, när de stängs, ser ut som om de är väggar. De specialdesignade möblerna gjordes i lackat rosenträ.

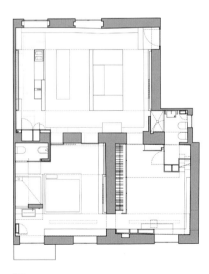

Plan

TOP-RECOLETA RENTAL

MARIANA BISCHOF
© Germán Falke

This apartment in Buenos Aires is located in a traditional residential building in the neighborhood of Recoleta. Originally used as a family home, it was remodeled and redecorated to create a rental property for foreign tourists visiting the city.

Cet appartement de Buenos Aires est situé dans une maison traditionnelle du quartier de Recoleta. Destinée à l'origine à l'usage exclusif d'une seule famille, cette habitation a été transformée et redécorée afin de proposer un hébergement de qualité aux touristes étrangers visitant la ville.

Dieses Appartement befindet sich in einem traditionellen Wohngebäude im Stadtteil Recoleta in Buenos Aires. Ursprünglich wurde es als Familienhaus genutzt, wurde dann aber umgebaut und neu gestaltet, um als Mietwohnung für ausländische Touristen der Stadt zu dienen.

Dit appartement in Buenos Aires bevindt zich in een traditioneel woongebouw in de wijk Recoleta. Aanvankelijk werd het gebruikt als gezinswoning. Later is het anders ingedeeld en opnieuw ingericht om verhuurd te worden aan buitenlandse toeristen die de stad bezoeken.

Este apartamento porteño, situado en un edificio residencial tradicional del barrio de Recoleta y originariamente utilizado como casa de familia, fue remodelado y redecorado para convertirlo en un piso de alquiler para turistas extranjeros en la ciudad de Buenos Aires.

Questo appartamento di Buenos Aires, situato in un edificio residenziale tradizionale nel quartiere di Recoleta e in origine utilizzato come abitazione familiare, è stato completamente ristrutturato e decorato in modo da poter essere affittato a turisti stranieri in visita alla città.

Este apartamento, situado num edifício tradicional do bairro de Recoleta e originalmente utilizado como habitação familiar em Buenos Aires, foi remodelado e redecorado para ser transformado num andar de aluguer para turistas estrangeiros na cidade Argentina.

Denna lägenhet i Buenos Aires är belägen i ett traditionellt hyreshus i området Recoleta. Ursprungligen användes huset som ett familjehem, men byggdes om och reparerades för att skapa en hyresfastighet för utländska turister som besöker staden.

GAMA-ISSA HOUSE

MARCIO KOGAN
© Arnaldo Pappalardo

The climate in this region is suitable for a house with a very open design. The large sliding windows which make up the wall create this openness to the exterior. The outside of the property is white, which reflects the light during the day. The inside is also white, with high book cases and modern furnishings.

Le climat de cette région est propice pour une maison de conception très ouverte. Les grandes baies coulissantes qui constituent le mur créent précisément cette ouverture sur l'extérieur. La résidence est de couleur blanche, qui réfléchit la lumière pendant la journée. L'intérieur est également blanc, avec de hautes bibliothèques et du mobilier moderne.

Das Klima der Region erlaubte ein offenes Wohndesign. Die großen Schiebefenster in der Wand unterstreichen diese Offenheit gegenüber dem Außenraum. Die weiße Außenfarbe verleiht dem Haus tagsüber Glanz. Auch im Innenraum dominiert die weiße Farbe, auffallend sind die hohen Bücherregale und das moderne Mobiliar.

Het klimaat in deze streek is geschikt voor een huis met een open karakter. De grote glazen schuifdeuren die de pui vormen, zorgen voor deze openheid. De witte buitenkant weerkaatst het zonlicht en houdt het huis koel. Ook het interieur is wit, met hoge boekenkasten en moderne meubels.

Gracias al clima de la región se pudo proyectar una vivienda muy abierta. Las grandes ventanas correderas que hacen de pared facilitan esta apertura al exterior. El exterior pintado de blanco hace que la casa durante el día sea muy brillante. En el interior destaca también el blanco, las estanterías altas para libros y el moderno mobiliario.

Grazie al clima della regione è stato possibile progettare una casa molto esposta; tale apertura all'esterno è favorita dalla presenza di grandi finestre scorrevoli che fanno anche da parete. Gli esterni dipinti di bianco fanno sì che durante il giorno la casa sia molto luminosa. Anche all'interno domina il bianco, nelle mensole alte per i libri e nell'arredamento moderno.

O clima da região permitiu projectar uma casa muito aberta. As grandes janelas corrediças que fazem de parede facilitam esta abertura ao exterior. A parte de fora pintada de branco faz com que a casa seja muito brilhante durante o dia. No interior também se destaca o branco, as estantes altas para livros e o mobiliário moderno.

Klimatet i denna region lämpar sig för ett hus med mycket öppen design. De stora skjutfönstren, vilka utgör väggen, skapar denna öppenhet mot exteriören. Fastighetens utsida är vit, vilket reflekterar solljuset under dagen. Insidan är också vit med höga bokhyllor och modernt möblemang.

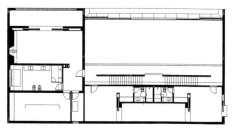

First floor

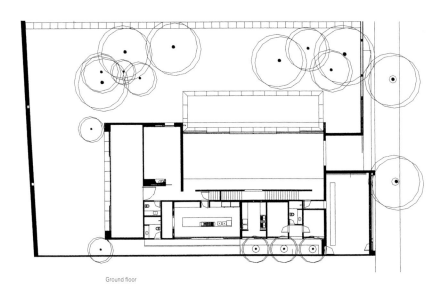

Ground floor

HOUSE IN **MIRAVALLE**

WOOD + ZAPATA
© Undine Pröh

The architects' main challenge with this project was that the house should have multiple views, so glass was used to create walls. Irregularity is the principal characteristic visible both inside and out, with a mixture of many different materials.

Le principal défiposé à l'architecte de ce projet était de ménager une multiplicité de vues – d'où l'utilisation de verre pour les murs. L'irrégularité est par ailleurs la principale caractéristique de cette réalisation, parfaitement visible au dedans comme au dehors, avec un mélange de nombreux matériaux différents.

Die Herausforderung der Architekten bestand bei der Planung des Projekts darin, dass das Haus möglichst viele verschiedene Ausblicke gewähren sollte, daher wurde Glas als Wandmaterial eingesetzt. Abwechslung ist die hervorragende Eigenschaft dieses Projekts, im Innen- und Außenraum kommt eine Vielfalt an Materialien zum Einsatz.

De grootste uitdaging voor de architect was het uitzicht te variëren. Daarom besloot hij de buitenmuren van glas te maken. Kenmerkend voor dit huis is de speelsheid, die ook tot uiting komt in het gebruik van veel verschillende materialen.

Cuando se planteó el proyecto, el principal desafío para los arquitectos era que la vivienda tuviera múltiples vistas, por lo que se recurrió al cristal a modo de pared. La irregularidad es la característica principal que se proyecta tanto en el exterior como en el interior, donde confluyen multiplicidad de materiales.

Quando si è lavorato a questo progetto, la sfida principale per gli architetti è consistita nella necessità di creare diverse viste nella casa, e per tale ragione si è deciso di fare ricorso al vetro concepito come parete. La caratteristica principale dell'edificio è la sua irregolarità, che si proietta tanto all'esterno quanto all'interno, dove confluiscono molteplici tipi di materiali.

Quando se concebeu este projecto, o principal desafio para os arquitectos era de que a vivenda tivesse múltiplas vistas, pelo que se recorreu ao cristal, para fazer de parede. A irregularidade é a característica principal que se projecta tanto no exterior como no interior, onde convergem muitos materiais.

Arkitektens huvudsakliga utmaning med detta projekt var att ge huset utsikt åt ett flertal håll. Därför användes glas till väggarna. Oregelbundenhet är den huvudsakliga karaktäristiken synlig både inom- och utomhus med en blandning av många olika material.

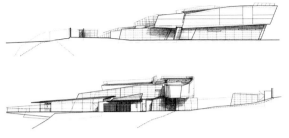

Elevations

Section

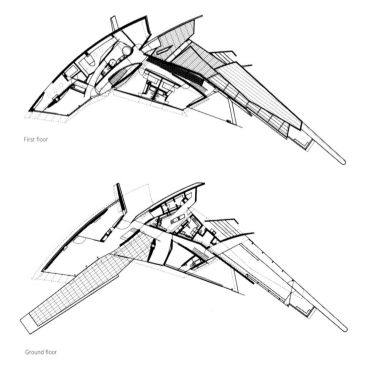

First floor

Ground floor

467

ABBOT KINNEY LOFTS

MARK MACK ARCHITECTS
© Undine Pröhl

Abbot Kinney is known as the artists' neighbourhood in California, so the project was to convert old houses into typical artists' lofts, creating somewhere with plenty of space in which they could both live and work. The three lofts share a façade and are separated by courtyards.

Abbot Kinney est connu comme le coin des artistes à Venice (Californie). Le projet était donc de transformer de vieilles maisons en véritables lofts, en créant des lieux spacieux où les artistes puissent vivre et travailler. Les trois lofts ont une façade commune ; à l'intérieur, ils sont séparés par des cours.

Der Stadtteil Abbot Kinney ist in Kalifornien als Künstlerviertel bekannt, daher mussten alte Wohnungen in für Künstler typische *lofts* umgestaltet werden: sie sollten Wohn- und Arbeitsraum in sich vereinen und über große Räume verfügen. Die drei *lofts* teilen dieselbe Fassade und sind durch Innenhöfe voneinander getrennt.

Abbot Kinney staat bekend als de artiestenbuurt van Californië. Het was dan ook de bedoeling oude huizen te veranderen in typische kunstenaarswoningen met voldoende ruimte voor een atelier. De drie lofts gaan schuil achter één gevel en zijn van elkaar gescheiden door binnenplaatsen.

El barrio Abbot Kinney se identifica por ser el barrio de los artistas en California, por lo que el proyecto debía convertir antiguas viviendas en típicos *lofts* de artista: posibilidad de trabajar y vivir en un mismo lugar y contar con amplios espacios. Los tres *lofts* comparten la fachada y se encuentran separados por patios.

Abbot Kinney è noto per essere il quartiere degli artisti in California; così il progetto doveva trasformare vecchie abitazioni in tipici *lofts* da artista: ossia luoghi in cui fosse possibile lavorare e vivere nonché avere a disposizione ampi spazi. I tre *lofts* condividono la facciata y e sono separati da cortili.

O bairro Abbot Kinney caracteriza-se por ser o bairro dos artistas na Califórnia, pelo que o projecto devia tornar vivendas antigas em típicos *lofts* de artista, permitindo assim trabalhar e viver num mesmo lugar e ter espaços amplos. Os três *lofts* compartilham as fachadas e estão separados por pátios.

Abbot Kinney är känt som konstnärskvarteren i Kalifornien, så projektet var att omvandla gamla hus till typiska konstnärsloft och på så sätt skapa ett ställe med got tom utrymme för både boende och arbete. De tre loften delar fasad och åtskiljs av innegårdar.

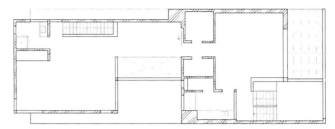

Second floor

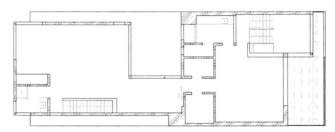

First floor

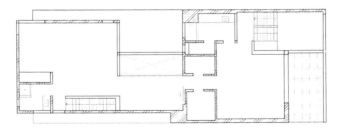

Ground floor

BAY CITIES LOFTS

MARK MACK ARCHITECTS
© Undine Pröh

The renovation of these lofts kept the original structure of the property, maintaining and highlighting the materials used in this kind of building. Wood, metal, brick and glass predominate, giving the house an industrial feel.

La rénovation de ces lofts a conservé la structure originale des lieux, en gardant et mettant en valeur les matériaux utilisés dans ce genre de bâtiment. Le bois, le métal, la brique et le verre prédominent, ce qui donne aux lofts un style industriel.

Bei der Renovierung dieser *Lofts* wurde die Originalstruktur des Gebäudes und seine charakteristischen Materialien erhalten. Holz, Metall, Ziegel und Glas sind bei diesem Haus vorherrschend und verleihen ihm seinen industriellen Charakter.

Tijdens de renovatie van deze bovenwoningen werd het oorspronkelijke karakter van het pand behouden door de materialen die bij gebouwen van dit type horen opnieuw te gebruiken. Hout, metaal, baksteen en glas geven het huis een industrieel karakter.

La reforma de estos *lofts* mantuvo la estructura original de la propiedad, manteniendo y destacando los materiales propios de este tipo de vivienda. La madera, el metal, el ladrillo y el cristal son los materiales predominantes que otorgan a la casa un carácter industrial.

La ristrutturazione di questi *lofts* ha conservato la struttura originale della proprietà, e ha valorizzato i materiali tipici di questo tipo di abitazione: il legno, il metallo, il mattone e il vetro che predominano e conferiscono alla casa un carattere industriale.

A reforma destes *lofts* manteve a estrutura original da propriedade, conservando e destacando os materiais próprios deste tipo de construção. A madeira, o metal, o tijolo e o cristal são os materiais predominantes que conferem à casa um carácter industrial.

Renoveringar av dessa vindsvåningar behöll fastighetens ursprungliga struktur; något som underhöll och underströk materialen som används i denna typ av byggnad. Trä, metal, tegel och glas dominerar vilket ger huset en industriell känsla.

480

Ground floor

First floor

Second floor

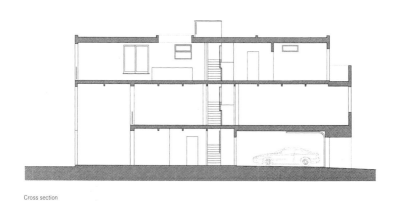

Cross section

TB GUEST LOFT

TOM MCCALLUM, SHANIA SHEGEDYN
© Shania Shegedyn

The challenge with this project was to transform an old photographic studio, located in a 19th century building, into an individual home. As the space to be restructured was small, a decision was made at the start to design the whole house with only the elements which were strictly necessary.

Le défide ce projet était de transformer un ancien studio photographique situé dans un bâtiment du XIXe siècle en appartement individuel. L'espace à restructurer étant restreint, la décision a été prise dès le départ de ne concevoir l'ensemble qu'avec les éléments strictement nécessaires.

Die Herausforderung bestand bei diesem Projekt darin, in einem Gebäude aus dem 19. Jahrhundert ein ehemaliges Fotostudio in eine Einzelwohnung umzugestalten. Da der zu gestaltende Raum begrenzt war, wurden von vornherein nur unbedingt notwendige Elemente in die Planung des Hauses einbezogen.

De architect stond voor de uitdaging een oude fotostudio, die in een 19e-eeuws gebouw was gevestigd, om te toveren in een woning. Omdat de te verbouwen ruimte beperkt was, besloot hij meteen het hele huis te ontwerpen, maar alleen met die elementen die strikt noodzakelijk waren.

El desafío de este proyecto consistió en transformar un antiguo estudio fotográfico, ubicado en un edificio del siglo XIX, en una vivienda unipersonal. Como el espacio a reestructurar era pequeño se decidió desde el principio proyectar y diseñar toda la casa sólo con los elementos estrictamente necesarios.

La sfida di questo progetto è stata quella di trasformare un vecchio studio fotografico, sito in un edificio del XIX secolo, in un'abitazione per una sola persona. Dal momento che lo spazio da ristrutturare era di piccole dimensioni, si è deciso fin dal principio di progettare tutta la casa solo con gli elementi strettamente necessari.

O desafio deste projecto consistiu em transformar um antigo estúdio fotográfico situado num edifício do século XIX numa casa unipessoal. Como o espaço a reestruturar era pequeno, decidiu-se desde o início projectar e desenhar a casa apenas com os elementos estritamente necessários.

Utmaningen med detta projekt var att omvandla en gammal fotostudio belägen i ett 1800-talshus till en privatbostad. Då ytan som skulle omvandlas var liten beslutades i början att huset endast skulle designas med de allra mest nödvändiga elementen.

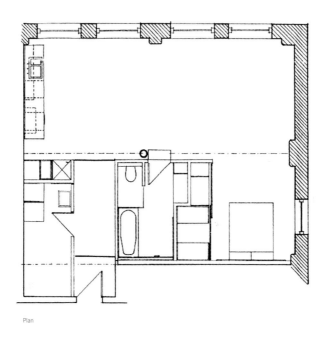

Plan

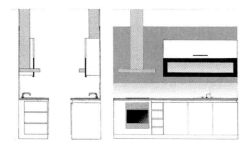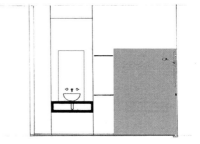

Interior elevations

SIBERIANA HOUSE

FILIPPO BOMBAC
© Luigi Fileti

The owners' Russian origins and their rich collection of contemporary art inevitably influenced the course of this project. The exclusive use of white produces a pleasant 'lunar' aspect, creating a certain Siberian feel.

Les origines russes des propriétaires et leur riche collection d'art contemporain ont logiquement influencé la conception de cette réalisation. L'usage exclusif du blanc engendre un plaisant aspect «lunaire» et crée par ailleurs une sorte d'ambiance sibérienne.

Die umfassende zeitgenössische Kunstsammlung der Eigentümer, und insbesondere die russische Herkunft des Käufers, haben bei diesem Projekt eine entscheidende Rolle gespielt. Durch die ausschließliche Verwendung von weißer Farbe wird ein ansprechendes Ambiente geschaffen, das an eine Mondlandschaft erinnert und zudem unverkennbar „sibirisch" wirkt.

De Russische afkomst van de eigenaren en hun rijke collectie hedendaagse kunst waren onvermijdelijk van invloed op de ontwikkeling van dit project. Het exclusieve gebruik van wit creëert een koele sfeer, die aan Siberië doet denken.

La rica colección de arte contemporánea de los propietarios, y especialmente los orígenes ruso del comprador, influyen inevitablemente en el curso de este proyecto. El uso exclusivo del colo blanco brinda un aspecto «lunar» muy agradable y otorga un aspecto inevitablemente «siberiano»

La ricca collezione d'arte contemporanea dei proprietari, e in particolar modo le origini russe dell'acquirente, hanno inevitabilmente influito sull'andamento di questo progetto. L'uso esclusivo del colore bianco offre un'atmosfera «lunare» molto gradevole e conferisce un aspetto immancabilmente «siberiano».

A rica colecção de arte contemporânea dos proprietários e, especialmente, as origens russas comprador influenciam inevitavelmente o percurso deste projecto. O uso exclusivo da cor bran oferece um aspecto "lunar" muito agradável e ao mesmo tempo inevitavelmente "siberiano".

Ägarnas ryska ursprung och deras rika samling av modern konst influerade ofrånkomligen det h projektets gång. Det exklusiva användandet av vitt skapar en behaglig "månkänsla", vilket ger speciell sibirisk känsla.

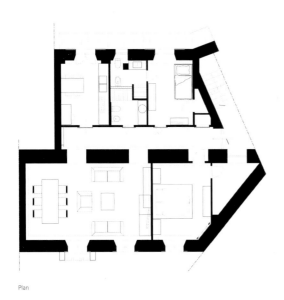

Plan

Section a-a'

Section b-b'

Section c-c'

Bedroom sketches